Weekly Reader:
SUMMER EXPRESS

New York • Toronto • London • Auckland • Sydney
Mexico City • New Delhi • Hong Kong • Buenos Aires

Editor: Ourania Papacharalambous
Cover design by Tannaz Fassihi and Michelle H. Kim
Interior design by Michelle H. Kim

ISBN: 978-1-338-10889-7
Compilation and illustrations copyright © 2017 by Scholastic Inc.
All rights reserved.
Printed in the U.S.A.
First printing, January 2017.

11 12 13   40   23 22 21

Table of Contents

Dear Parent,

Congratulations! You hold in your hands an exceptional educational tool that will give your child a head start in the coming school year.

Inside this book, you'll find 100 practice pages that will help your child review and learn the alphabet, numbers, colors, shapes, sorting, letters, sounds, and so much more! *Weekly Reader: Summer Express* is divided into 10 weeks, with two practice pages for each day of the week, Monday through Friday. However, feel free to use the pages in any order that your child would like. Here are other features you'll find inside:

★ A weekly incentive chart and certificate to motivate and reward your child for his or her efforts.

★ Ideas for fun, skill-building activities you can do with your child any time.

★ Suggestions for creative learning activities that you can do with your child each week.

★ A certificate of completion to celebrate your child's accomplishments.

We hope you and your child will have a lot of fun as you work together to complete this workbook.

Enjoy!

The Editors

Tips for Using This Book

1. Pick a good time for your child to work on the activities. You may want to do it around mid-morning after play, or early afternoon when your child is not too tired.

2. Make sure your child has all the supplies he or she needs, such as pencils and an eraser. Designate a special place for your child to work.

3. Have stickers handy as rewards. Celebrate your child's accomplishments by letting him or her affix stickers to the incentive chart after completing the activities each day.

4. Encourage your child to complete the worksheets, but don't force the issue. While you may want to ensure that your child succeeds, it's also important that he or she maintains a positive and relaxed attitude toward school and learning.

5. After you've given your child a few minutes to look over the activity pages he or she will be working on, ask your child to tell you his or her plan of action: "Tell me about what we're doing on these pages." Hearing the explanation aloud can provide you with insights into your child's thinking processes. Can he or she complete the work independently? With guidance? If your child needs support, try offering a choice about which family member might help. Giving your child a choice can help boost confidence and help him or her feel more ownership of the work to be done.

6. When your child has finished the workbook, present him or her with the certificate of completion on page 143. Feel free to frame or laminate the certificate and display it on the wall for everyone to see. Your child will be so proud!

Skill-Building Activities for Any Time

The following activities are designed to complement the 10 weeks of practice pages in this book. These activities don't take more than a few minutes to complete and are just a handful of ways in which you can enrich and enliven your child's learning. Use the activities to take advantage of time you might ordinarily disregard—for example, standing in line or waiting at a bus stop. You'll be working to practice key skills and have fun together at the same time.

Find Real-Life Connections

One of the reasons for schooling is to help children function in the real world, to empower them with the abilities they'll truly need. So why not put those developing skills into action by enlisting your child's help with creating a grocery list, reading street signs, sorting pocket change, and so on? He or she can apply reading, writing, science, and math skills in important and practical ways, connecting what he or she is learning with everyday tasks.

An Eye for Patterns

A red-brick sidewalk, a beaded necklace, a Sunday newspaper—all show evidence of structure and organization. You can help your child recognize the way things are structured, or organized, by observing and talking about patterns they see. Your child will apply his or her developing ability to spot patterns across all school subject areas, including alphabet letter formation (writing), attributes of shapes and solids (geometry), and characteristics of narrative stories (reading). Being able to notice patterns is a skill shared by effective readers and writers, scientists, and mathematicians.

Journals as Learning Tools

Most of us associate journal writing with reading comprehension, but having your child keep a journal can help you keep up with his or her developing skills in other academic areas as well—from telling time to matching rhymes. To get started, provide your child with several sheets of paper, folded in half, and stapled together. Explain that he or she will be writing and/or drawing in the journal to complement the practice pages completed each week. Encourage your child to draw or write about what he or she found easy, what was difficult, or what was fun. Before moving on to another set of practice pages, take a few minutes to read and discuss that week's journal entries together.

Promote Reading at Home

- Let your child catch you in the act of reading for pleasure, whether you like reading science fiction novels or do-it-yourself magazines. Store them someplace that encourages you to read in front of your child and **demonstrate that reading is an activity you enjoy.** For example, locate your reading materials on the coffee table instead of your nightstand.

- Set aside a family reading time. By designating a reading time each week, your family is assured an opportunity to discuss with each other what you're reading. You can, for example, share a funny quote from an article. Or your child can tell you his or her favorite part of a story. The key is to **make a family tradition of reading and sharing books** of all kinds together.

- **Put together collections of reading materials** your child can access easily. Gather them in baskets or bins that you can place in the family room, the car, and your child's bedroom. You can refresh your child's library by borrowing materials from your community's library, buying used books, or swapping books and magazines with friends and neighbors.

Skills Alignment

Listed below are the skills covered in the activities throughout *Weekly Reader: Summer Express*. These skills will help children review what they know while helping prevent summer learning loss. They will also better prepare each child to meet, in the coming school year, the math and language arts learning standards established by educators.

Math

	Week 1	Week 2	Week 3	Week 4	Week 5	Week 6	Week 7	Week 8	Week 9	Week 10
Know number names and the count sequence.	✦	✦	✦	✦	✦	✦	✦	✦	✦	✦
Count to tell the number of objects.	✦	✦	✦	✦	✦	✦	✦	✦	✦	✦
Compare numbers.	✦	✦	✦	✦						
Understand addition as putting together and adding to.		✦			✦		✦	✦		✦
Understand subtraction as taking apart and taking from.				✦		✦	✦			
Work with numbers 11–19 to gain foundation for place value.								✦		✦
Describe and compare measurable attributes.							✦		✦	
Classify objects and count the number of objects in categories.			✦						✦	✦
Identify and describe shapes.						✦	✦	✦		
Analyze, compare, create, and compose shapes.								✦		✦

Language Arts

	Week 1	Week 2	Week 3	Week 4	Week 5	Week 6	Week 7	Week 8	Week 9	Week 10
Ask and answer questions about key details.				✦	✦	✦	✦	✦	✦	✦
Retell familiar stories, including key details.								✦		✦
Identify the main topic and retell key details in a text.					✦		✦		✦	
Identify characters, settings, and major events in a story.			✦		✦	✦			✦	
Ask and answer questions about unknown words.								✦	✦	
Recognize common types of texts.		✦			✦					
Describe relationships between illustrations and the text.		✦	✦				✦			
Compare and contrast characters in a story.			✦							
Identify similarities and differences between two texts on the same topic.									✦	
Demonstrate understanding of the organization and basic features of print.	✦	✦	✦	✦	✦	✦	✦	✦	✦	✦
Demonstrate understanding of spoken words, syllables, and sounds.	✦	✦	✦	✦			✦			
Know and apply grade-level phonics and word analysis skills in decoding words.	✦	✦	✦	✦	✦	✦	✦	✦	✦	✦
Tell about the events in the order in which they occurred.						✦		✦	✦	
Confirm understanding of a text read aloud or information presented orally or through other media.		✦	✦	✦	✦	✦	✦	✦	✦	✦
Demonstrate command of the conventions of standard English grammar and usage when writing or speaking.	✦					✦		✦		
Demonstrate command of the conventions of standard English capitalization, punctuation, and spelling.	✦	✦	✦	✦	✦	✦	✦	✦	✦	✦
Explore word relationships.						✦				✦

Help Your Child Get Ready: Week 1

Here are some activities that you and your child might enjoy.

Laundry Sort
When putting away the laundry, enlist your child's help in sorting and matching the socks.

Odd (and Even) Houses
As you go for a stroll, point out street addresses in your neighborhood. Guide your child to notice house numbers on one side of the street and compare them with house numbers on the other side. Ask your child what he or she notices about these numbers.

Labels, Labels Everywhere
Label different items in your child's room using sticky notes. Encourage your child to read the labels and to help you write some of the labels as well.

Let's Go to the Library
Visit your local library and encourage your child to select a few picture books to borrow.

These are the skills your child will be working on this week.

Math
- number sequence through 10
- count to 5
- connect numbers to quantities
- count objects in groups
- differentiate more vs. fewer

Handwriting
- numbers 1–10

Foundational Skills
- match upper- and lowercase letters
- alphabetical order

Phonics
- initial consonants
- identify words that rhyme
- recognize words with short *a*

Incentive Chart: Week 1

Week 1	Day 1	Day 2	Day 3	Day 4	Day 5
Put a sticker to show you completed each day's work.	☆ ☆	☆ ☆	☆ ☆	☆ ☆	☆ ☆

CONGRATULATIONS!

Wow! You did a great job this week!

This certificate is presented to:

_____

_____   _____

Date   Parent/Caregiver's Signature

Letter Friends

Help these letters find their friends. Draw a line to match each uppercase letter with its lowercase letter.

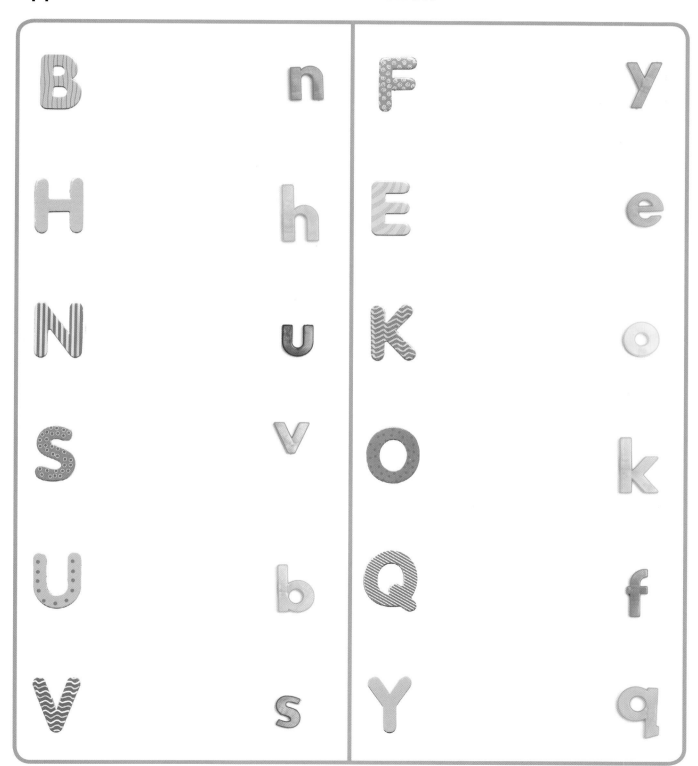

Letter Friends

Help these letters find their friends. Draw a line to match each uppercase letter with its lowercase letter.

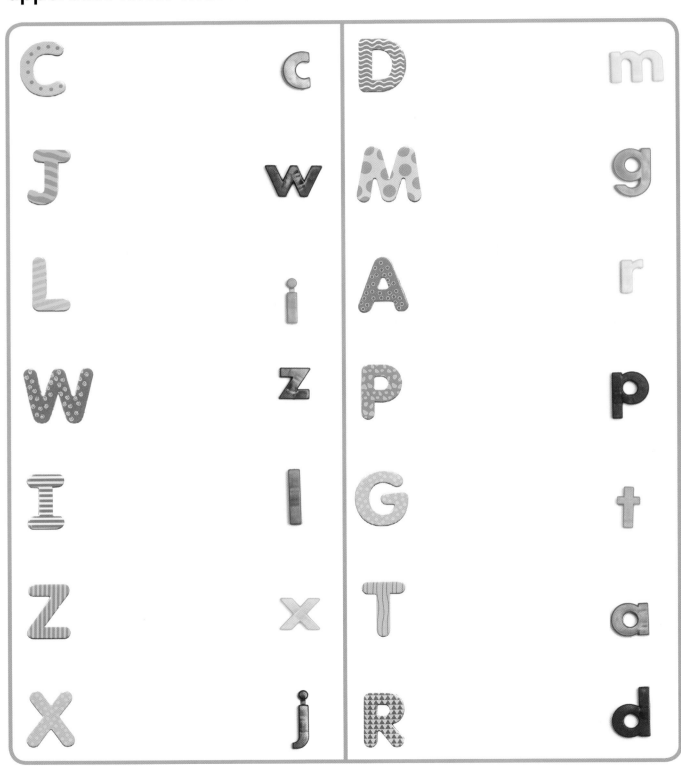

Count Across Our Country

Count. Then write the number on the line.

There are _____ seashells on the beach.

There are _____ bison on the plain.

There are _____ cacti in the desert.

There are _____ trees in the prairie.

What's the Missing Number?

Some of the number blocks are missing numbers! Fill in the missing numbers. Then print the numbers one to ten below.

Match Me!

Draw a line from each picture to its beginning sound.

c

b

l

t

p

m

d

f

Fill-In Rhymes

**Rhyming words sound alike. Read the rhyme.
Circle the rhyming pictures to finish the poem.**

One **1**, two **2**,
buckle my

Three **3**, four **4**,
knock at the

Five **5**, six **6**,
pick up

Seven **7**, eight **8**,
lay them straight

Nine **9**, ten **10**,
a good fat

 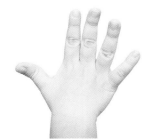

What's the Scoop?

Count the scoops on each ice cream cone.
Write the number on the cone.

1. Circle the cone with the fewest scoops.

2. Put an ✖ on two cones with an equal number of scoops.

3. Put a ✔ on the cone with the most chocolate scoops.

4. How many scoops of ice cream are there in total? _____

How Many Fish?

Count the fish in each bowl. Write the number in the box.
Then, in each set, circle the bowl that has more.

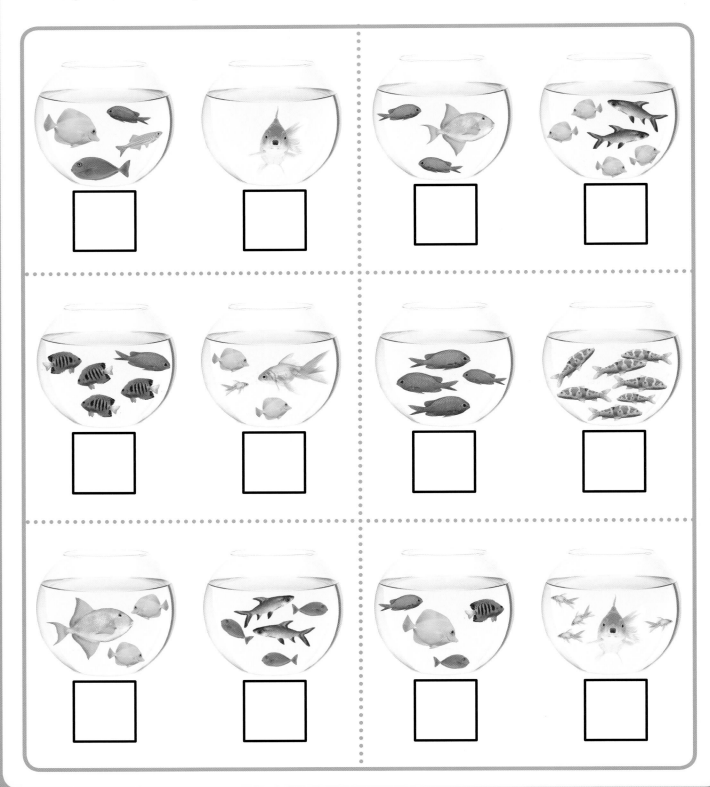

Short-*a* Words

Some words have the short-*a* sound, like *cat*.
Look at the pictures. Say the words. Listen to the short-*a* sound.
Underline the short *a* in each word.

bat   mask   lamp

fan   jam   map

Look at the words above. Write them in the boxes.

Words With 3 Letters
_____
_____
_____
_____

Words With 4 Letters
_____
_____
_____
_____

A Snack for the Cats

The cats like snacks with the short-*a* sound. Look at the pictures in each box. Say the words. Listen for the short-*a* sound. Circle the snacks each cat likes best.

Help Your Child Get Ready: Week 2

Here are some activities that you and your child might enjoy.

How Many in Our Family?

Make counting more meaningful to your child by asking: *How many feet are there in our family? How many eyes? How many fingers in our family?*

Letter Collection

With your child, collect items that start with a particular letter. For example, you might take a book, a ball, and a bell, and put them all in a box labeled *B*.

High-Frequency Words

High-frequency words, or sight words, occur frequently in the English language. Since many of these words do not follow regular phonetic rules, it is important that your child can recognize them on sight. When reading with your child, point to sight words such as *the, of, to, you, she, my, is, are, do,* and *does.* Say the word and have your child repeat after you. Then point to the word again and have your child say it and use it in a sentence.

How Long Is a Minute?

Help your child get a better sense of how long a minute is. Challenge your child to do an activity, such as jumping rope or balancing on one foot, while timing him or her for one minute.

These are the skills your child will be working on this week.

Math

- match numbers to number words
- connect numbers to quantities
- interpret graphs
- read a pictograph
- number sequence to 15

Handwriting

- number words

Phonics

- high-frequency word *the*
- understand letter-sound correspondences
- identify words that rhyme
- recognize words with short *e*
- word family: *-est*

Incentive Chart: Week 2

Week 2	Day 1	Day 2	Day 3	Day 4	Day 5
Put a sticker to show you completed each day's work.	☆ ☆	☆ ☆	☆ ☆	☆ ☆	☆ ☆

CONGRATULATIONS!

Wow! You did a great job this week!

This certificate is presented to:

_____

_____   _____
Date   Parent/Caregiver's Signature

Sight Word: *the*

Trace and write *the* on the line.

_____

the

Find each leaf that has *the*. Trace the path from that leaf to the basket.

Write the missing letters to spell *the*.

Circle the two socks in each set with the letters that spell *the*.

Rhyme Time!

Write a letter in the blank space to make a rhyming pair.

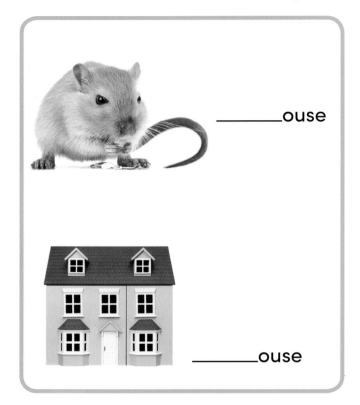

_____ouse

_____ouse

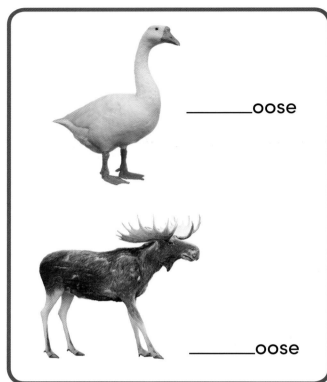

_____oose

_____oose

_____oat

_____oat

_____ug

_____ug

Marble Match

Draw a line to match each number to its number word.

 1 •   • two

2 •   • three

3 •   • one

4 •   • five

5 •   • four

6 •   • seven

7 •   • eight

8 •   • six

9 •   • ten

10 •   • nine

Count the Sleeping Animals!

Count the animals. Write the number and the number word.

Number Key					
1	2	3	4	5	6
one	two	three	four	five	six

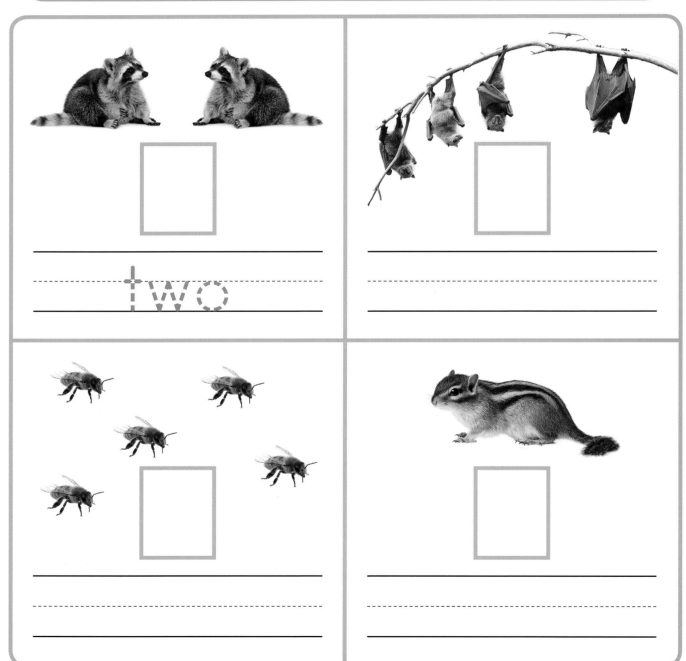

two

Short-e Words

Some words have the short-*e* sound like *ten*.
Look at the pictures. Say the words. Listen to the short-*e* sound.
Underline the short *e* in each word.

bed	bell	hen
nest	net	tent

Look at the words above. Write them in the boxes.

Words With 3 Letters	**Words With 4 Letters**
_____	_____
_____	_____
_____	_____

Hen's Nest

Hen likes the short-*e* sound. Say the names for the pictures in each box. Listen for the short-*e* sound. Circle the short-*e* pictures.

The Best Nest

Read the poem.
Underline all the words that end with -est.

If you see a robin's nest,
It is best to let it rest.
Do not ever be a pest,
Just let that bird's nest rest!

Look at Robin in her nest,
Folded wings across her chest.
She protects her eggs the best,
In her little nest.

Peck—an eggshell gets a test.
One egg's hatching before the rest.
CRACK! It's open! That's the best—
A new chick's in the nest!

How Many Eggs?

This graph shows how many eggs each bird laid in its nest.

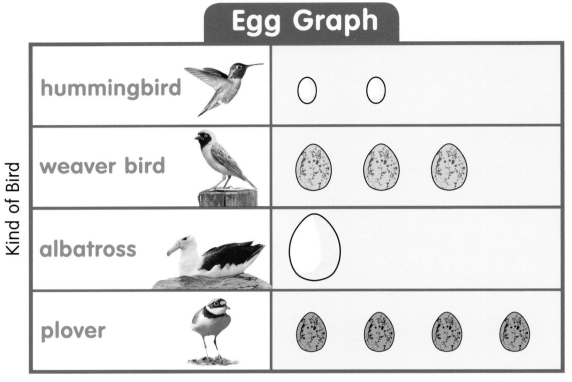

Read each question. Circle the correct answer.

1. How many eggs did the 🐦 lay?　　1　　2　　3　　4

2. How many eggs did the 🐦 lay?　　1　　2　　3　　4

3. How many eggs did the 🐦 lay?　1　　2　　3　　4

4. Which bird laid more eggs?

You Can Count on Me!

Count. Then fill in the blanks.

1 I have ⬜ letters in my name.

2 I am ⬜ years old.

3 There are ⬜  in my home.

people

4 There are ⬜  in my home.

windows

5 There are ⬜  in my home.

chairs

I Can Count to 15!

Write the missing numbers.

9, 10, 11, 12, _____, 14, _____

Count the number of objects in each box and circle that number.

| 15 | 14 | 11 | 12 | 14 | 13 | 11 | 14 | 13 |

**Apples sometimes fall from trees.
Draw 15 apples on the ground.**

Help Your Child Get Ready: Week 3

Here are some activities that you and your child might enjoy.

Funny Business

Read a simple comic strip with your child. Then, cut apart the strip into individual frames and have your child put them back in order.

Audio Books

Record yourself reading one of your child's favorite books. Keep the book and recording accessible so that your child can play the recording and follow the words in the book.

Flip It!

Take a deck of playing cards and remove all the jacks, queens, and kings. Distribute the cards evenly between you and your child, making sure to keep the cards facedown. When you say, "Flip it!" both you and your child flip the top card from your pile at the same time. Whoever gets the higher number shouts, "Mine!" and keeps both cards. The person who collects the most cards at the end of the game wins.

Kitchen Words

Have a set of magnetic letters available for your child to use in the kitchen, on the refrigerator. While you prepare a meal, encourage your child to use the magnetic letters to spell the colors or names of items you are using at the moment.

These are the skills your child will be working on this week.

Math
- identify patterns
- addition within 8
- connect numbers to quantities
- number sequence through 20

Reading
- make connections between illustrations and a text
- identify characters in a story

Phonics
- high-frequency word *of*
- understand letter-sound correspondences
- recognize words with short *i*

Incentive Chart: Week 3

Week 3	Day 1	Day 2	Day 3	Day 4	Day 5
Put a sticker to show you completed each day's work.	☆	☆	☆	☆	☆

CONGRATULATIONS!

Wow! You did a great job this week!

This certificate is presented to:

_____

_____   _____

Date   Parent/Caregiver's Signature

Number Pattern

Write the numbers to complete each pattern.

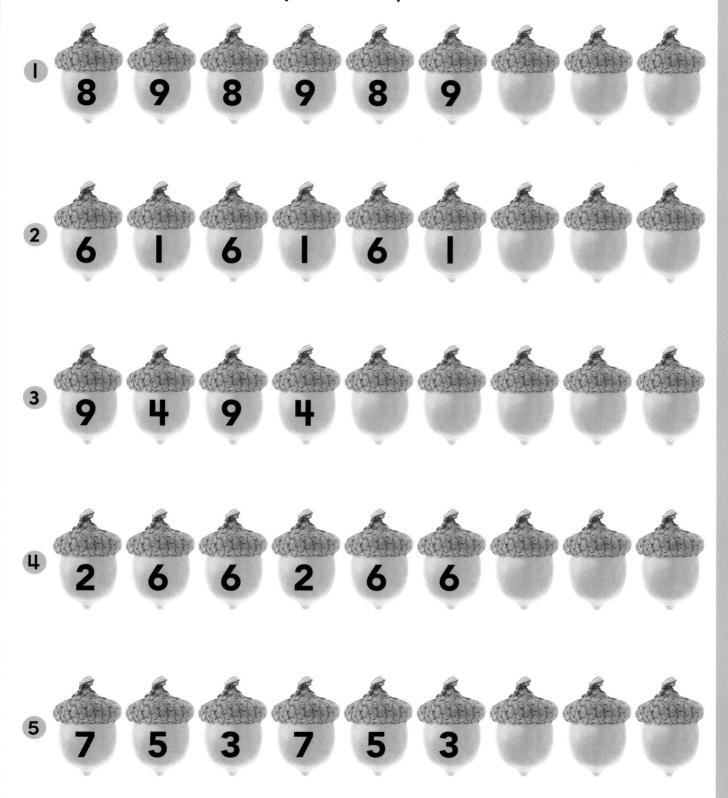

1. 8 9 8 9 8 9 _ _ _

2. 6 1 6 1 6 1 _ _ _

3. 9 4 9 4 _ _ _ _ _

4. 2 6 6 2 6 6 _ _ _

5. 7 5 3 7 5 3 _ _ _

How Many More Make 5?

Draw more eggs so that each nest has 5.
Then finish the number sentence.

3 + _____ = 5

2 + _____ = 5

1 + _____ = 5

4 + _____ = 5

Sight Word: *of*

Trace and write *of* on the line.

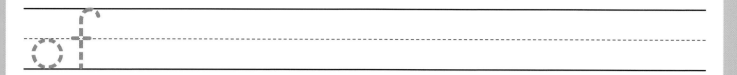

Draw a line from each duck to the puddle that has *of*.

off

of

of

to

on

of

Write *of* on each duck.

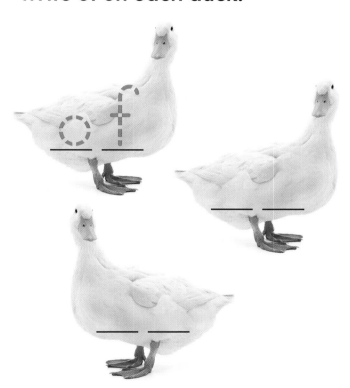

Circle each duckling that has *of*.

of   off   of   of   to

Off the Log

Read. Then write the names of the frogs in the picture.

Two frogs sit on a log.

"I will hop off," says one.

"I will swim off," says the other.

Hank hops. Suzy swims.

Who is Hank? Who is Suzy?

Tentacles and Legs

Finish the ocean animals.
Then complete each number sentence.

Draw tentacles so each jellyfish has 5.

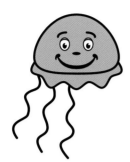 

3 + ___ = 5   4 + ___ = 5

Draw arms so each octopus has 8.

 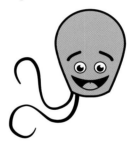

5 + ___ = 8   2 + ___ = 8

Draw legs so each crab has 6.

2 + ___ = 6   3 + ___ = 6

Count the Objects

Count the correct number of objects.
Draw an X through the extra objects.

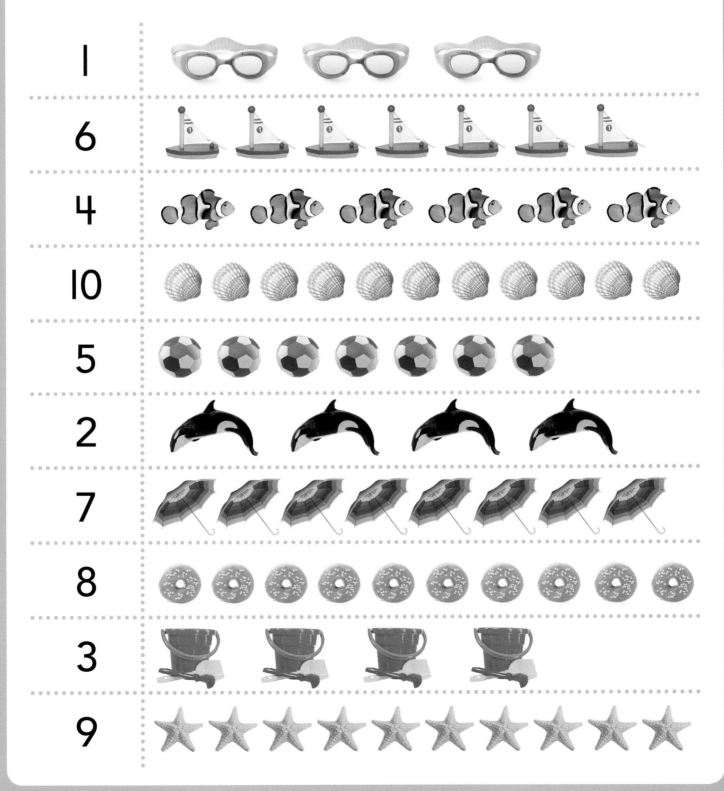

1

6

4

10

5

2

7

8

3

9

Short-*i* Words

Some words have the short-*i* sound like *six*.
Say the name for each picture. Listen to the short-*i* sound.
Underline the short *i* in each word.

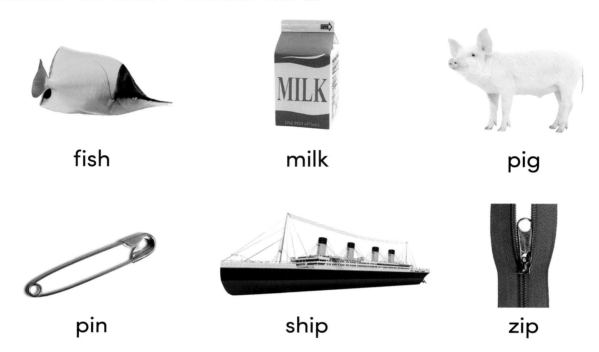

fish   milk   pig

pin   ship   zip

Look at the words above. Write them in the boxes.

Words With 3 Letters	Words With 4 Letters
_____	_____
_____	_____
_____	_____

Pig's Picture

Pig takes pictures of the short-*i* sound.
Say the name for each picture. Listen
for the short-*i* sound. Circle the word,
then write it.

fox   fish

_____

show   ship

_____

soap   sink

_____

milk   make

_____

Counting Windows

Write the missing numbers.

1		3	4	
6		8	9	
11	12		14	
	17			20

I Can Count to 20!

Write the missing numbers.

15, 16, _____, _____, 19, _____

Count the number of objects in each box and circle that number.

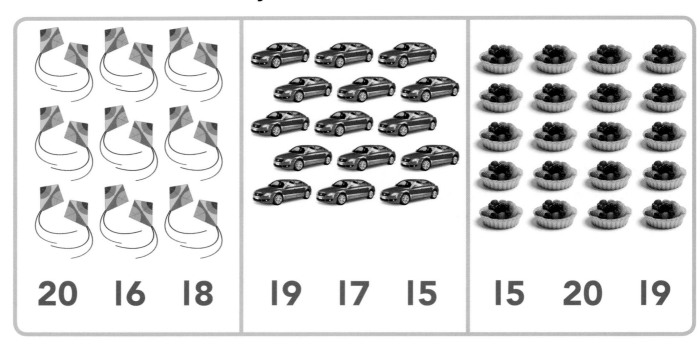

| 20 | 16 | 18 | | 19 | 17 | 15 | | 15 | 20 | 19 |

Draw 20 stars in the space below.

Help Your Child Get Ready: Week 4

Here are some activities that you and your child might enjoy.

Measuring With String

Give your child a shoestring and have him or her look for objects that are longer than the string, then for objects that are shorter than the string.

Picture a Story

Have your child search for an intriguing picture from a newspaper or magazine. Encourage him or her to tell a story about the picture. For example, if it's a picture of a whale breaching from the water, your child might say it's about a whale wanting to fly in the air.

Money Matters

If you have a collection of loose coins, enlist your child's help in sorting, counting, and wrapping the coins to deposit in the bank.

Family Names

Together with your child, write down the names of family members and friends. You can then count the number of letters in each name, or count the number of times a particular letter appears in the list of names and create a graph.

These are the skills your child will be working on this week.

Math

- differentiate more vs. fewer
- connect numbers to quantities
- subtraction within 8
- number sequence through 30

Reading

- answer questions about a text

Phonics

- high-frequency word *to*
- understand letter-sound correspondences
- identify words that rhyme
- beginning sounds
- recognize words with short *o*

Incentive Chart: Week 4

Week 4	Day 1	Day 2	Day 3	Day 4	Day 5
Put a sticker to show you completed each day's work.	☆ ☆	☆ ☆	☆ ☆	☆ ☆	☆ ☆

CONGRATULATIONS!

Wow! You did a great job this week!

This certificate is presented to:

_____

_____ _____
Date   Parent/Caregiver's Signature

Sight Word: *to*

Trace and write *to* on the line.

Find each coin that has *to*. Trace the path from that coin to the bank.

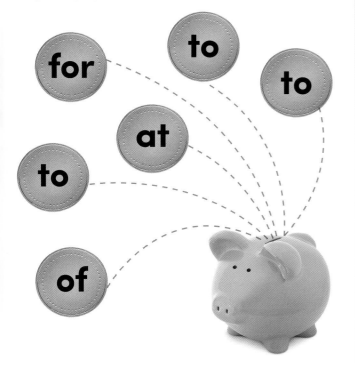

Write *to* on each tent.

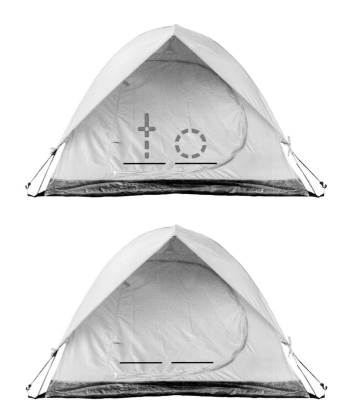

Circle each block with the word *to*.

Rhyme Time!

Choose a letter from the box to complete each rhyming pair.

h   g   c   b   w   p

a __f__ox in a ___ox

a ___oat in a ___oat

a ___at in a ___at

a ___ig in a ___ig

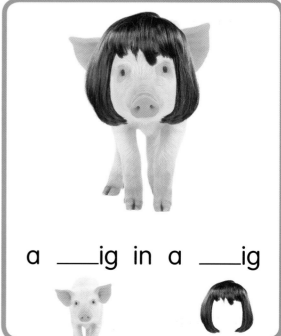

Red, White, and Blue!

Count the objects in each group. Then write the number in the box below. Finally, circle the group that has more.

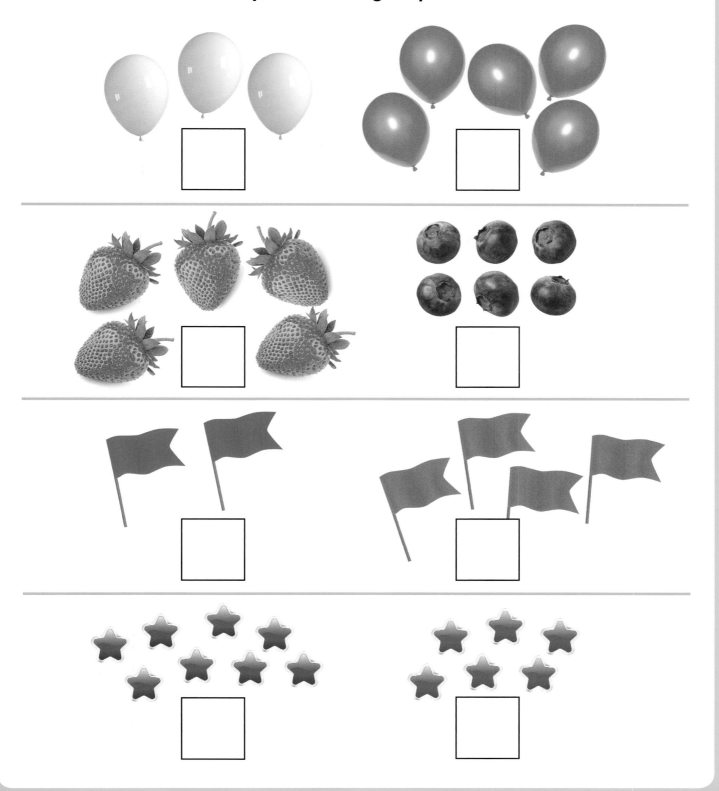

Let's Count

Count the correct number of objects.
Draw an X through the extra objects.

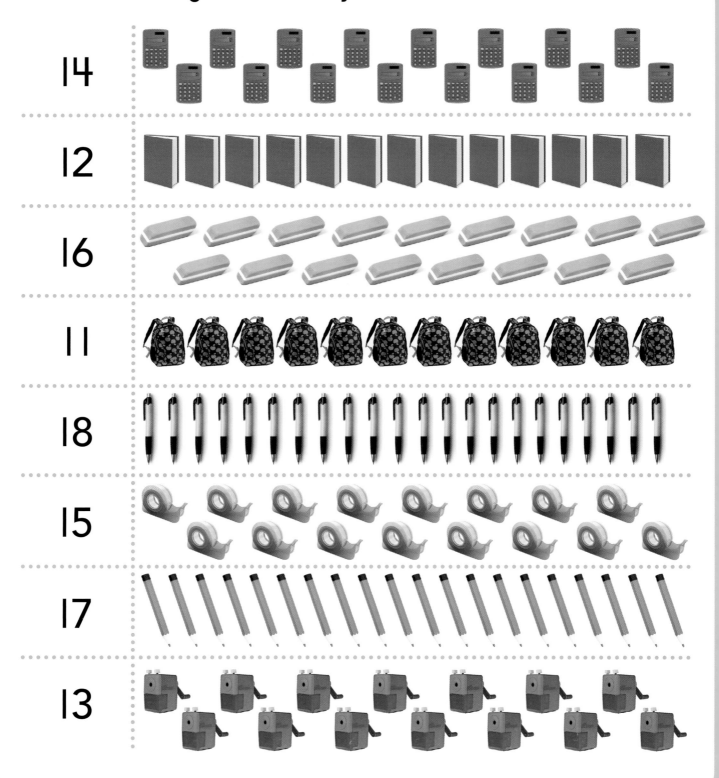

Ants Came to Our Picnic!

What did they carry away?
Choose a letter from the box to complete each word.

p	a	w	i	b	f	c	ch

____ork

____pple

____izza

____orn

____anana

____atermelon

____ce cream

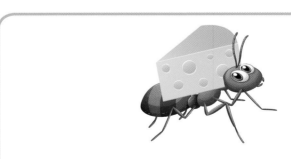

Challenge: _____eese

Wally the Whale

Read the story. Then read each sentence.
Is the sentence true or false? X the correct box.

Wally is a big blue whale. Wally lives in the ocean. He swims with his whale friends. Sometimes Wally dives deep, then he jumps high into the air. When he lands in the water, Wally makes a big splash.

1 Wally is a red whale.

☐ True   ☐ False

2 Wally lives in the ocean.

☐ True   ☐ False

3 Wally swims alone.

☐ True   ☐ False

4 Wally dives deep.

☐ True   ☐ False

5 When Wally lands in the water, he makes a splash.

☐ True   ☐ False

Back From the Beach

Write the answer for each problem.
Then use the code to answer the question.

n 7 – 2 = ☐

e 6 – 3 = ☐

r 8 – 1 = ☐

i 8 – 0 = ☐

m 7 – 1 = ☐

d 8 – 4 = ☐

f 5 – 3 = ☐

o 8 – 8 = ☐

t 3 – 2 = ☐

What will you hear when you walk into the house?

Use the code to find out.

$$\frac{}{1} \ \frac{}{8} \ \frac{}{6} \ \frac{}{3} \qquad \frac{}{2} \ \frac{}{0} \ \frac{}{7}$$

$$\frac{}{4} \ \frac{}{8} \ \frac{}{5} \ \frac{}{5} \ \frac{}{3} \ \frac{}{7} !$$

A Race to the Finish Line

Help Charlie and Jennifer reach the finish line.
Fill in the missing numbers along the path.

Short-*o* Words

Some words have the short-*o* sound like *sock*.
Say the name for each picture. Listen to the short-*o* sound.
Underline the short *o* in each word.

box   doll   fox

sock   stop   top

Look at the words above. Write them in the boxes.

Words With 3 Letters	Words With 4 Letters
_____	_____
_____	_____
_____	

A Toy Box for Fox

Fox's favorite toys have the short-*o* sound. Look at the pictures. Say the words. Listen for the short-*o* sound. Circle the word, then write it.

boat   block

_____

frog   flag

_____

tent   top

_____

doll   duck

_____

Help Your Child Get Ready: Week 5

Here are some activities that you and your child might enjoy.

Shopping for Consonants

While at the grocery store, pick a consonant letter and challenge your child to find and call out items that begin with that letter sound.

Graphing

Have your child create a graph. If indoors, use a bowl with a variety of fruit or a bag of colorful candy. If in the yard or on the patio, direct your child to observe the different colors of the flowers. Have your child graph the number of each color seen. For example, *two red flowers* and *ten yellow flowers*. You may want to give your child a sheet of graph paper on which to create the graph.

Fun With Fonts

Let your child experiment on the computer with different fonts of the same letter.

Moon Mania

Track the phases of the moon with your child for a month. (You don't have to go out every night.) Encourage your child to draw the shape of the moon each time you see it. After a few days, have your child predict what shape he or she will see the next night.

These are the skills your child will be working on this week.

Math

- skip count by 2s
- addition within 10
- number sequence through 50
- match numbers to number words

Reading

- identify key details
- describe connections within a text

Phonics

- high-frequency word *you*
- understand letter-sound correspondences
- recognize words with short *u*

Incentive Chart: Week 5

Week 5	Day 1	Day 2	Day 3	Day 4	Day 5
Put a sticker to show you completed each day's work.	☆ ☆	☆ ☆	☆ ☆	☆ ☆	☆ ☆

CONGRATULATIONS!

Wow! You did a great job this week!

This certificate is presented to:

_____

_____ _____
Date　　　　　　　　　　　Parent/Caregiver's Signature

Summer Skip Counting

1 Count the bikes' wheels by 2s. There are ☐ wheels in all.

2 Count the paddles by 2s. There are ☐ paddles in all.

3 Count the ears by 2s. There are ☐ ears in all.

4 Count the flip flops by 2s. There are ☐ flip flops in all.

How Many More Beach Balls?

Draw a beach ball in each empty box to make 10 beach balls.
Then complete the equation.

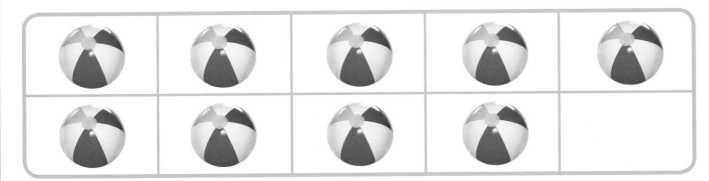

$$9 + \underline{\hspace{2cm}} = 10$$

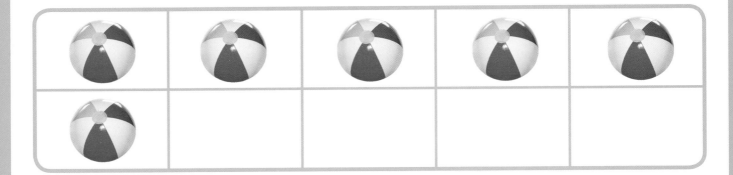

$$6 + \underline{\hspace{2cm}} = 10$$

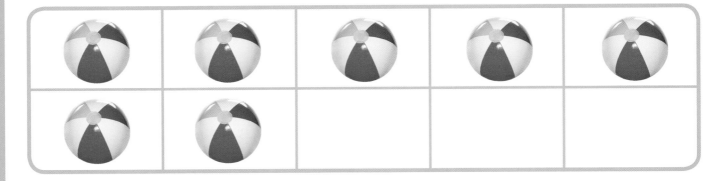

$$7 + \underline{\hspace{2cm}} = 10$$

Sight Word: *you*

Trace and write *you* on the line.

you

Find each kite that has *you*. Trace the path from that kite to the child.

Write the missing letters to spell *you*.

Y _ _ _

_ O _

Circle each acorn that has *you*.

you put you

use you

Alexander Graham Bell

Read the article and the chart. Then answer the questions.

Alexander Graham Bell grew up in Scotland. He learned to play the piano. He also liked to make new things.

Alexander wanted to make sound travel. He needed to make a new machine. It was hard work. In 1876, he did it! Alexander Graham Bell invented the telephone. Thomas Watson helped him.

Telephones Through the Years

1876   1964   1992

1 Who invented the telephone? Circle the name.

2 Who helped invent the telephone? Underline the name.

3 Circle the telephone from 1964.

4 What phone do you use today? Draw a picture.

An Ocean Code

First, solve these math problems.

```
    2          2          6          2
  + 3        + 1        + 1        + 2
  ┌───┐      ┌───┐      ┌───┐      ┌───┐
  └───┘      └───┘      └───┘      └───┘
    V          W          S          A
```

```
    1          1          3
  + 1        + 0        + 3
  ┌───┐      ┌───┐      ┌───┐
  └───┘      └───┘      └───┘
    T          I          E
```

Now put the letters in the correct space below. You will find the answer to a joke!

How can you tell that the ocean is friendly?

___ ___   ___ ___ ___ ___ ___ !
 1   2   3   4   5   6   7

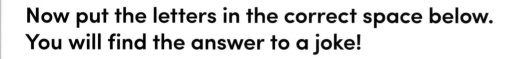

How Many Fish?

Count the fish in each set. Write the number in the box.

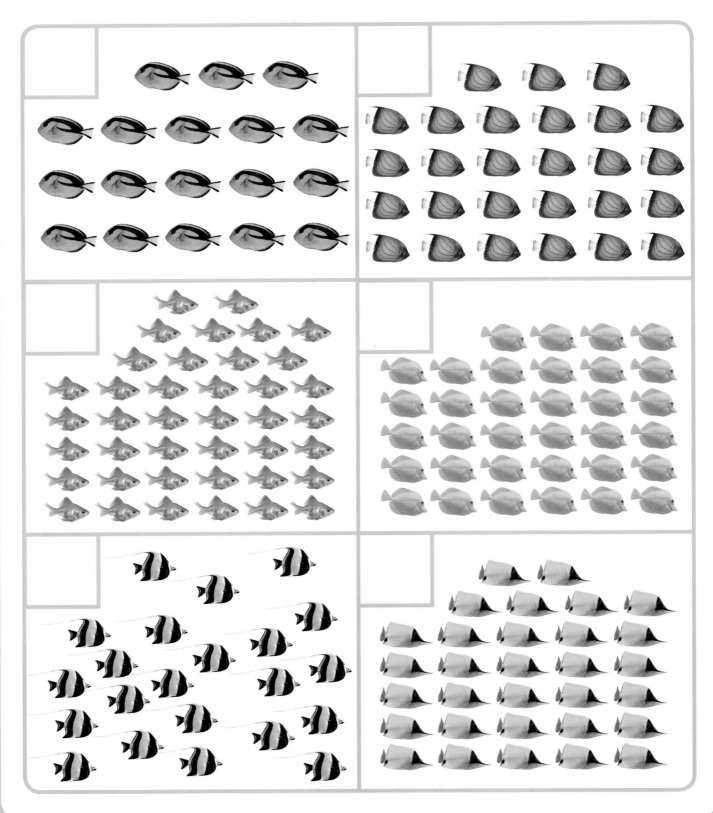

Short-*u* Words

Some words have the short-*u* sound like *sun*.
Say the name for each picture. Listen to the short-*u* sound.
Underline the short *u* in each word.

bus   drum   duck

rug   skunk   truck

Look at the words above. Write them in the boxes.

Words With 3 Letters

_____   _____

Words With 4 Letters

_____   _____

Words With 5 Letters

_____   _____

Bug's Busy Day

Bug had a busy day! Say the name for each picture. Circle the word, then write it. Use the words to tell a story about Bug's busy day.

up   cup

_____

run   bun

_____

juggle   just

_____

tub   tug

_____

Matching Numbers

Draw a line to match each number to its number word.

11 •   • thirteen

12 •   • fifteen

13 •   • twelve

14 •   • eighteen

15 •   • eleven

16 •   • fourteen

17 •   • seventeen

18 •   • sixteen

19 •   • twenty

20 •   • nineteen

Big Bowl of Jellybeans

Draw 50 jellybeans inside the bowl. Use the colors shown.
Then answer the question below.

How many jellybeans did you draw in each color?
Write the number.

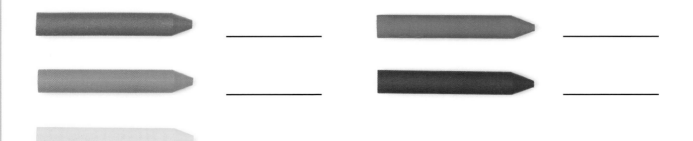

Help Your Child Get Ready: Week 6

Here are some activities that you and your child might enjoy.

"I Spy" a Rhyme

Play an "I Spy" rhyming game with your child in your house or while walking around the neighborhood. For example, "I spy something that rhymes with bee." (*tree*)

Bath Time Measurements

Supply your child with measuring cups and spoons in the bathtub. Have him or her explore the relationship between different tools of measurement. For example, your child can investigate how many tablespoons of water fit in one cup.

Order in the Kitchen

Write a simple recipe (such as making instant pudding) on index cards, one step per card. Read each step to your child. Then mix up the steps and ask your child to put the recipe back together in order. Then make the recipe with your child.

Word Search

Look for a long word, such as *caterpillar*, and challenge your child to find shorter words within the word.

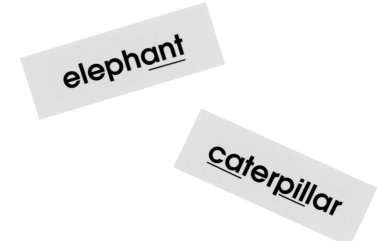

These are the skills your child will be working on this week.

Math

- analyze and compare shapes
- subtraction within 10
- classify objects
- number sequence through 60

Foundational Skills

- understand word relationships

Reading

- identify the main idea
- describe setting
- draw conclusions

Phonics

- high-frequency word *she*
- understand letter-sound correspondences
- ending consonants
- recognize words with long *a* and long *i*

Incentive Chart: Week 6

Week 6	Day 1	Day 2	Day 3	Day 4	Day 5
Put a sticker to show you completed each day's work.	☆ ☆	☆ ☆	☆ ☆	☆ ☆	☆ ☆

CONGRATULATIONS!

Wow! You did a great job this week!

This certificate is presented to:

_____

_____ _____
Date   Parent/Caregiver's Signature

Sight Word: *she*

Trace and write *she* on the line.

Trace each flower that has *she*.

Write the missing letters to spell *she*.

Circle each set of bags with the letters that spell *she*.

Lunch Buddies

Read the story, then answer the questions.

Roger was feeling a little sad. It was the first day of school, and he had no one to eat lunch with. Roger saw a new boy who looked sad, too.

"Is something wrong?" Roger asked.

"I forgot to bring my lunch money," said the boy.

"I have a big lunch," said Roger, "Why don't you sit with me? Then we can share."

1 This story is mostly about
○ forgetting lunch.
○ feeling hungry.
○ finding a lunch buddy.

2 Where does this story take place?
○ at school
○ at Roger's home
○ on the playground

3 What do you think will happen the next day?
○ The new boy will forget his money.
○ The boys will sit together.
○ The boys will both feel sad.

What Shape Am I?

Draw a line from each picture to its matching shape.

square

oval

diamond

rectangle

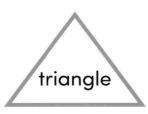
triangle

circle

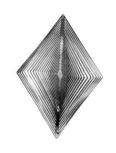

Take It Away

Solve each problem. Cross out objects to help you subtract.
Write each answer.

1

8 – 2 = _____

5

6 – 4 = _____

2

5 – 1 = _____

6

10 – 5 = _____

3

9 – 2 = _____

7

7 – 7 = _____

4

10 – 9 = _____

8

5 – 2 = _____

Match My Sounds!

Draw a line from each picture to its ending sounds.

 g

 r

 m

 p

 t

 n

 d

x

One Word Out

Some words belong together
Because they are alike.
Words like *seat*, *wheels*, and *pedals*
Are all part of my bike.

Big, *large*, and *huge*
Are words that mean the same.
Tag, *jump rope*, and *hopscotch*
Are all kinds of fun games.

Let's see if you can choose
The word that does not fit
In each group of words below:
Just find and circle it!

①	yellow	blue	four	red
②	I	me	your	my
③	warm	cold	many	hot
④	down	seven	six	eight
⑤	run	walk	jump	laugh
⑥	to	blue	two	too
⑦	say	play	over	may

Graph the Garden

Look at the garden.
Color one box in the graph for each item you see.

Garden Graph

Garden Item					
carrot 🥕	1	2	3	4
worm 〰️	1	2	3	4
ladybug 🐞	1	2	3	4
flower 🌼	1	2	3	4

Number of Items

How Many Are There?

Count the objects in each set. Write the number in the box.

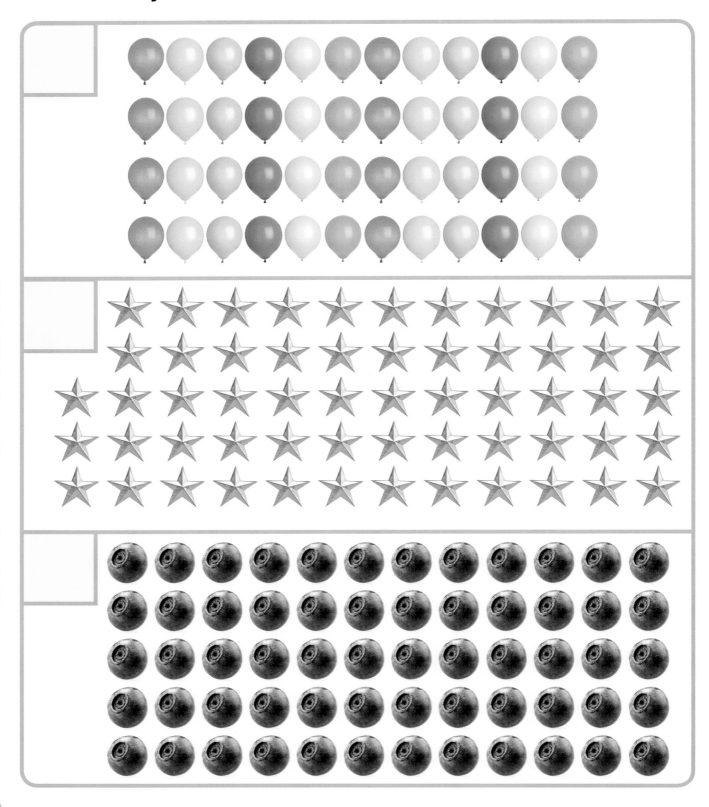

Silent-e Words

A vowel can sound like its name. This is called a long-vowel sound. Look at the pictures. Say the words. Listen for the sound of *a* and *i*. Underline *a* and *i*.

| bike | cake | gate |

| kite | mice | rake |

Look at the words above. Write them in the boxes.

Words With Long *a*	Words With Long *i*
_____	_____
_____	_____
_____	_____

Long or Short?

Circle each picture with a long-vowel sound.

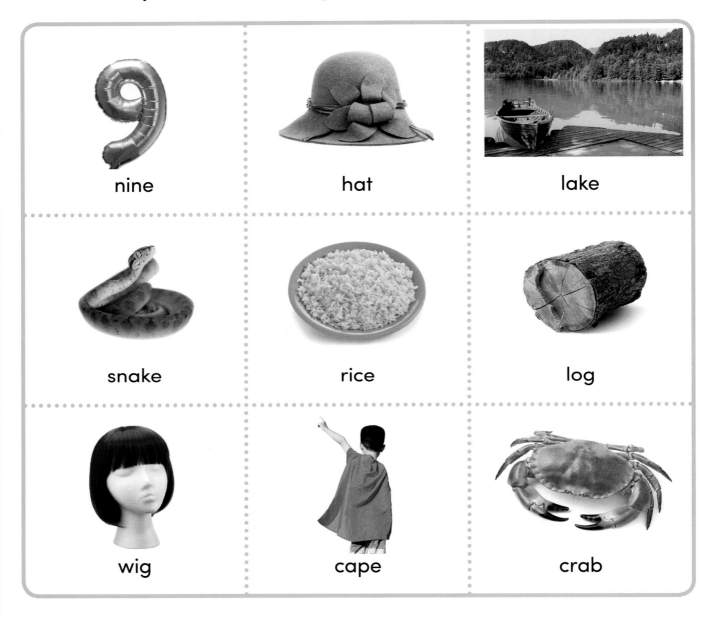

nine	hat	lake
snake	rice	log
wig	cape	crab

Add a letter to complete the name of each object.

c_____ke   b_____ke

Help Your Child Get Ready: Week 7

Here are some activities that you and your child might enjoy.

Weighty Investigations

Ask your child, "Do you think a cup of cotton balls weighs the same as a cup of paper clips?" Give your child two same-size paper cups and fill one with cotton balls and the other with paper clips. Have your child hold a cup in each hand and tell you which one is heavier. Encourage your child to think of other items to compare.

Go Right, I Mean, Left!

Hide a toy in a room for your child to find. Bring your child into the room and call out direction words, such as *left* or *right*, to help your child move toward the toy. Then switch places with your child.

Rock Candy

Make candy crystals with your child. Heat up ½ cup of water until it boils. Little by little, add one cup of sugar into the water until no more sugar will dissolve. Then add some food coloring. When the liquid has cooled down a bit, carefully pour it into a glass. Place a wooden craft stick into the glass and set it aside in a place where it will be undisturbed. With your child, observe the glass and stick every day and watch as sugar crystals grow.

Magnetic Story

Invite your child to create a short sentence, poem, or story on the refrigerator using magnetic letters or words.

These are the skills your child will be working on this week.

Math

- differentiate fewer vs. more
- subtraction within 10
- solve word problems
- number sequence through 70
- analyze and compare shapes
- addition within 10

Reading

- main idea and details
- make connections between illustrations and a text

Phonics

- high-frequency word *my*
- understand letter-sound correspondences
- recognize words with long *o* and long *u*
- distinguish between long and short vowel sounds

Incentive Chart: Week 7

Week 7	Day 1	Day 2	Day 3	Day 4	Day 5
Put a sticker to show you completed each day's work.	☆ ☆	☆ ☆	☆ ☆	☆ ☆	☆ ☆

CONGRATULATIONS!

Wow! You did a great job this week!

This certificate is presented to:

_____

_____   _____
Date   Parent/Caregiver's Signature

Fewer or More

Fill in the blank to make the sentence true. Use fewer or more.

24 teeth

0 teeth

1 An elephant has

_____

teeth than a turtle.

34 teeth

80 teeth

2 A camel has

_____

teeth than an alligator.

30 teeth

42 teeth

3 A cat has

_____

teeth than a dog.

98 teeth

36 teeth

4 A dolphin has

_____

teeth than a hippo.

Math Problem of the Day

Use the cups to solve each problem.

9 – _____ = 5   6 – _____ = 5

Use the number line to solve each problem.

1 2 3 4 5 6 7 8 9 10

1 8 – 5 = _____   4 10 – 8 = _____

2 6 – 4 = _____   5 2 – 1 = _____

3 5 – 3 = _____   6 7 – 2 = _____

Sight Word: *my*

Trace and write *my* on the line.

Circle each section that has *my*.

yes · any · my · my · my · by · why · my

Write *my* on each bucket.

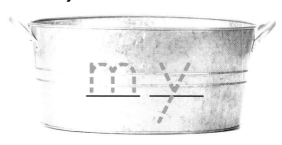

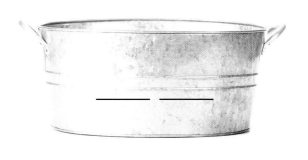

Draw a line from each bee to the hive that has *my*.

my · at

to · my

by · my

Snakes Are Everywhere!

Read the article. Then answer the questions.

Some snakes live in forests. Some live in hot, dry deserts. Others live in lakes or streams. Some snakes even live in the sea! Snakes live almost everywhere. But they never live where it is always freezing cold.

1. What is the paragraph about?
   - ○ where snakes live
   - ○ what snakes eat
   - ○ how snakes move

2. In which of these places do snakes never live?
   - ○ forests
   - ○ deserts
   - ○ where it is always cold

3. Where does the snake in the photo most likely live?
   - ○ a forest
   - ○ a desert
   - ○ a lake or stream

Word Problems

Draw a picture to solve each problem.
Write the number sentence on the line.

1 Lori picked up four acorns. Then she picked up three more acorns. How many acorns does Lori have?

_____

2 Dennis planted two apple seeds and seven pumpkin seeds. How many seeds did Dennis plant in all?

_____

3 George made 10 cookies. Then he ate six of the cookies he made. How many cookies does George have left?

_____

All About Baseball

Draw a line to match each number to the set with the same number of objects.

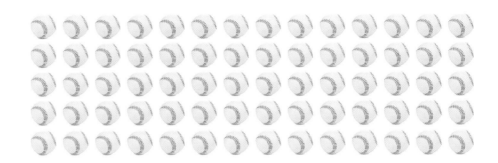

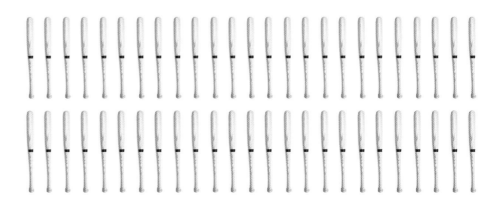

More Silent-*e* Words

A vowel can sound like its name. This is called a long-vowel sound. Look at the pictures. Say the words. Listen for the sound of *o* and *u*. Underline *o* and *u*.

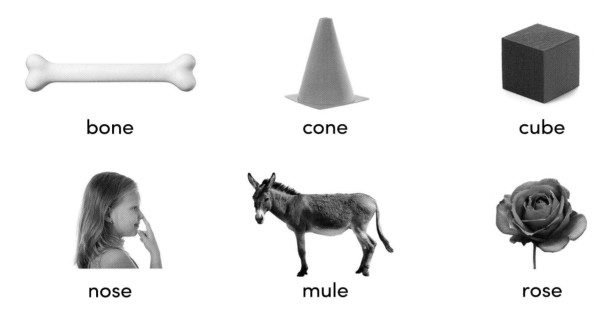

bone

cone

cube

nose

mule

rose

Look at the words above. Write them in the boxes.

Words With Long *o*
_____
_____
_____
_____

Words With Long *u*
_____
_____
_____
_____

No Bones About It

**Find the long-vowel word to complete each sentence.
Circle that bone.**

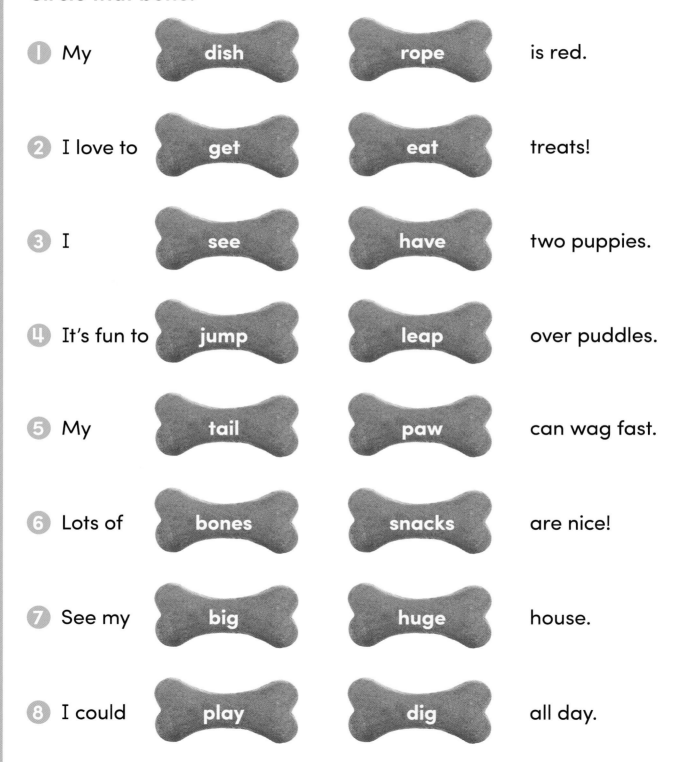

1 My **dish** **rope** is red.

2 I love to **get** **eat** treats!

3 I **see** **have** two puppies.

4 It's fun to **jump** **leap** over puddles.

5 My **tail** **paw** can wag fast.

6 Lots of **bones** **snacks** are nice!

7 See my **big** **huge** house.

8 I could **play** **dig** all day.

Frame It!

Look at the shape of each frame.
Circle the pictures with the same shape.

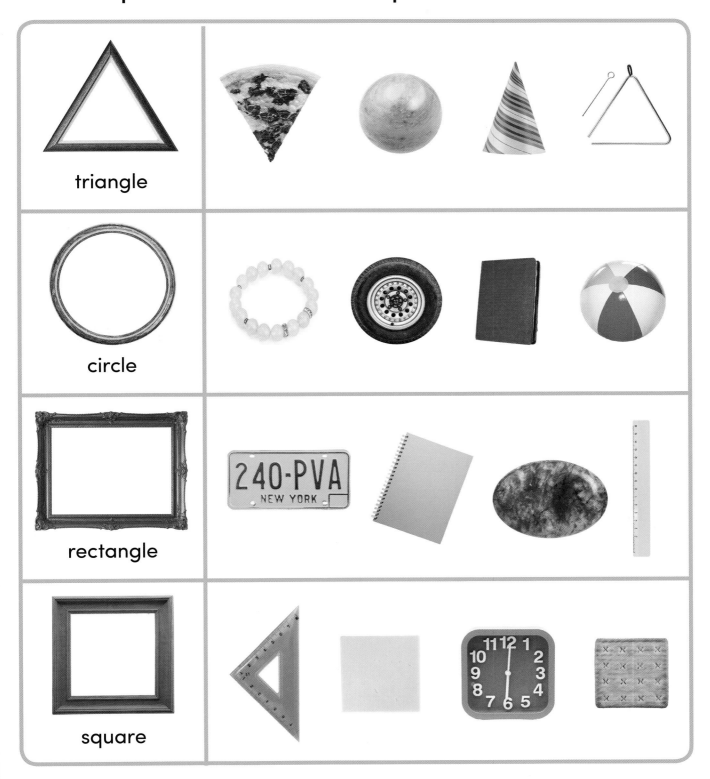

triangle

circle

rectangle

square

240-PVA
NEW YORK

Word Problems

Austin, Jim, Michelle, and Diane each wants to bring fruit to share with their 10 classmates. Each child has packed some fruit in their bag already. How many more pieces does each child need?

Draw pictures to help solve the problem.
Then write the number on the line to complete the equation.

Austin	Jim
8 + _____ = 10	_____ + 7 = 10
Michelle	Diane
5 + _____ = 10	_____ + 4 = 10

Help Your Child Get Ready: Week 8

Here are some activities that you and your child might enjoy.

Cereal Sorting

After breakfast, engage your child in a sorting activity using multicolored cereal. Invite your child to sort the cereal by shape or by color.

Riddle Me This

Play a consonant riddle game with your child. Say a word, then challenge your child to find a rhyming word that starts with a given sound. For example, "What rhymes with *run* and starts with *f*?"

Funny Names

Encourage your child to create a story starring a character with a silly rhyming or alliterative name, such as Funny Bunny, Matt the Cat, or Dilly Duck.

Menu Math

While having dinner at a restaurant, encourage your child to explore the prices on the menu. Ask questions such as, "How many items do you see that cost less than $10? What's the most expensive item on this menu? What's the least expensive item? How much do french fries cost?"

These are the skills your child will be working on this week.

Math
- identify relative position
- draw shapes
- addition within 15
- number sequence through 80

Handwriting
- color words

Reading
- answer questions about a text
- context clues

Phonics
- high-frequency word *is*
- understand letter-sound correspondences
- count syllables in a word
- beginning and ending consonants

Grammar
- form plurals

Incentive Chart: Week 8

Week 8	Day 1	Day 2	Day 3	Day 4	Day 5
Put a sticker to show you completed each day's work.	☆ ☆	☆ ☆	☆ ☆	☆ ☆	☆ ☆

CONGRATULATIONS!

Wow! You did a great job this week!

This certificate is presented to:

_____

_____   _____
Date   Parent/Caregiver's Signature

Sight Word: *is*

Trace and write *is* on the line.

Circle each pair of jellybeans with the letters that spell *is*.

Write *is* on each block.

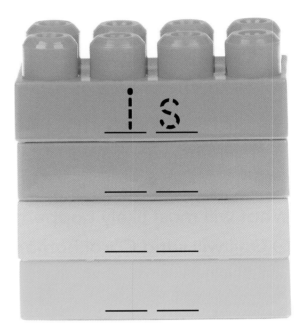

Circle each part of the snake that has *is*.

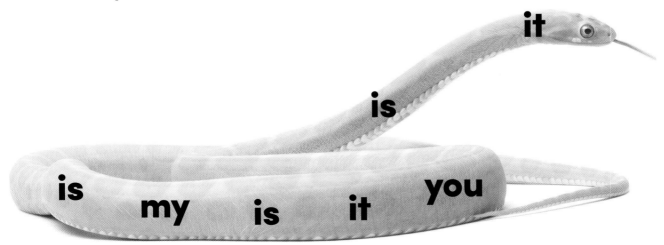

The Forgotten Panda

Read the story. Then answer the questions.

Each morning Gail walks Carol, her little sister, to school. She holds Carol's hand. Gail makes sure Carol gets to her classroom safely. Today Carol is crying. She is **upset**.

Why? Carol forgot her panda for show-and-tell. Gail cannot get her sister to stop crying.

① What will most likely happen next?
- ○ Gail will send Carol home to get the panda.
- ○ Gail will leave Carol on the sidewalk crying.
- ○ Gail will take Carol home to get the panda.

② What can you tell about Gail from this story?
- ○ Gail is a good sister.
- ○ Gail forgot Carol.
- ○ Gail forgot the panda.

③ In this story, what does the word **upset** mean?
- ○ knock over
- ○ unhappy
- ○ upside down

Relative Position

Circle the term that best describes the dog's position in each photo.

1 above   below

2 in front of   behind

3 next to   behind

4 inside   outside

Shapely Addition

Review shapes.

Draw three ovals.

Draw two rectangles.

Use the number line to solve each problem.

3 4 5 6 7 8 9 10 11 12

❶
$\begin{array}{r} 4 \\ + 6 \\ \hline \end{array}$

❷
$\begin{array}{r} 5 \\ + 7 \\ \hline \end{array}$

❸
$\begin{array}{r} 9 \\ + 2 \\ \hline \end{array}$

❹
$\begin{array}{r} 8 \\ + 3 \\ \hline \end{array}$

❺
$\begin{array}{r} 6 \\ + 6 \\ \hline \end{array}$

❻
$\begin{array}{r} 3 \\ + 6 \\ \hline \end{array}$

I Spy Animals

Play "I Spy Animals." Say the name of the animals in each box. Clap and count the syllables for each. Circle the animal that matches the number of syllables listed in each box.

Begin and End With Consonants

Read the letter in each row. Fill in the circle next to each picture whose name begins with that sound.

1 n   ○   ○   ○

2 d   ○   ○   ○

3 f   ○   ○   ○

Read the letter in each row. Fill in the circle next to each picture whose name ends with that sound.

4 k   ○   ○   ○

5 s   ○   ○   ○

6 t   ○   ○   ○

Count the Cookies

Look at the number on each jar. Count the cookies in each set.
Draw a line to match the cookies to the jar with the same number.

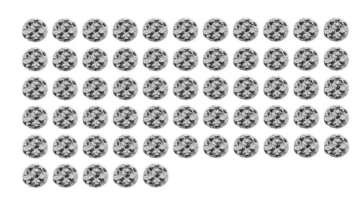

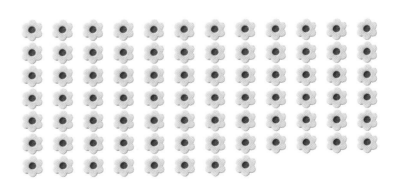

More Shapely Addition

Review shapes.

Draw five squares.

Draw four triangles.

Use the number line to solve each problem.

| 6 | 7 | 8 | 9 | 10 | 11 | 12 | 13 | 14 | 15 |

1.   7
   + 7
   ___

2.   8
   + 5
   ___

3.   7
   + 8
   ___

4.   9
   + 3
   ___

5.   6
   + 7
   ___

6.   9
   + 6
   ___

Animal Facts

Write *s* on the lines. Then, read the sentences.

Zebra__ have lot__ of stripe__.

Frog__ eat lot__ of bug__.

Leopard__ have lot__ of spot__.

And teddy bear__ give hug__!

Fun Phonics

Circle the word that names each picture.

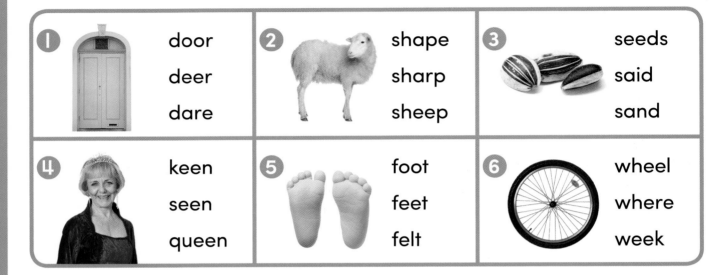

1	door	2	shape	3	seeds
	deer		sharp		said
	dare		sheep		sand
4	keen	5	foot	6	wheel
	seen		feet		where
	queen		felt		week

Color Words

Trace. Then write.

red

pink

green

yellow

Help Your Child Get Ready: Week 9

Here are some activities that you and your child might enjoy.

Rhyming Pictures

Give your child some old magazines and a pair of safety scissors. Then, ask your child to cut out pictures of things whose names rhyme, such as *bat* and *hat*, or *coat* and *boat*.

Puzzling Sentences

Write a sentence on a strip of paper, leaving lots of room between the words. For example: *Carlos is reading his favorite book*. Cut the words apart and put them in an envelope. Have your child put the words together to form a sentence.

Neighborhood Map

While walking with your child, take pictures of different "landmarks" in your neighborhood, such as your own home, the grocery store, the mailbox, dry cleaners, playground, and so on. Then create a large map of the neighborhood with your child using the photographs to indicate different places.

Cereal Math

Use candy or cereal to help reinforce the concept of addition and subtraction. For example, say, "If I have two pieces of cereal and you have one, how many do we both have?" Help your child count the total number of pieces.

These are the skills your child will be working on this week.

Math

- interpret graphs
- addition and subtraction within 10
- use a graph to classify objects
- identify patterns
- compare size
- number sequence through 90

Reading

- main idea and details
- compare and contrast
- sequence

Phonics

- high-frequency word *are*
- understand letter–sound correspondences
- beginning and ending consonants

Incentive Chart: Week 9

Week 9	Day 1	Day 2	Day 3	Day 4	Day 5
Put a sticker to show you completed each day's work.	☆☆	☆☆	☆☆	☆☆	☆☆

CONGRATULATIONS!

Wow! You did a great job this week!

This certificate is presented to:

_____

_____   _____
Date   Parent/Caregiver's Signature

Seed Graph

Read the graph. Then (circle) the correct answers.

Type of Fruit							
orange	1	2	3	4	5	6	
apple	1	2	3	4	5	6	
cucumber	1	2	3	4	5	6	
lemon	1	2	3	4	5	6	

Number of Seeds

1 How many seeds are in the ?   **2**   **3**

2 How many seeds are in the  ?   **5**   **6**

3 How many seeds are in the ?   **6**   **7**

4 Circle the one that has more seeds?

Blast Off

Add or subtract. Then use the code to answer the riddle below.

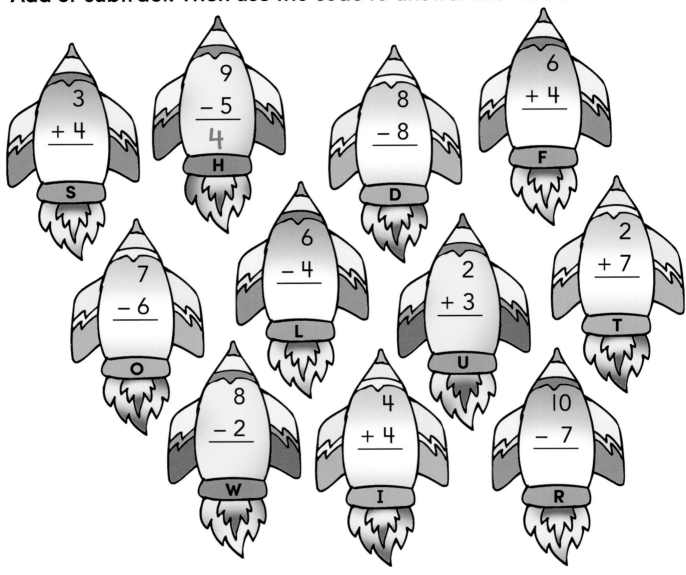

3
+ 4
___
S

9
− 5
___
4
H

8
− 8
___
D

6
+ 4
___
F

7
− 6
___
O

6
− 4
___
L

2
+ 3
___
U

2
+ 7
___
T

8
− 2
___
W

4
+ 4
___
I

10
− 7
___
R

How is an astronaut's job unlike any other job?

___ ___ ___ , ___   ___ ___ ___   ___ ___
8   9   7   7   1   5   9   1   10

___ H ___ ___   ___ ___ ___ ___ ___ ___!
9   4   8   7   6   1   3   2   0

Sight Word: *are*

Trace and write *are* on the line.

_____

are

_____

Help each crow get to the corn. Connect the dots to spell *are*. Start at *a*.

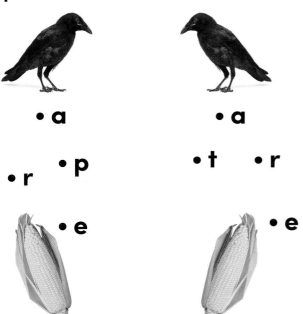

Write the missing letters to spell *are*.

Circle each train car that has *are*.

are   ate   are   and   are   ate

Whales and Elephants

**Animals are amazing! Read each paragraph.
Answer the questions.**

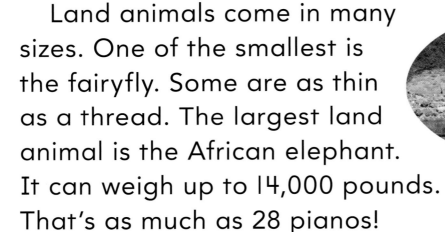

The ocean is full of animals. The smallest are called zooplankton. Some ocean animals are huge! The largest is the blue whale. It can grow to be 100 feet long!

Land animals come in many sizes. One of the smallest is the fairyfly. Some are as thin as a thread. The largest land animal is the African elephant. It can weigh up to 14,000 pounds. That's as much as 28 pianos!

1 What are both paragraphs about?

○ animals   ○ land animals   ○ ocean animals

2 How are the paragraphs different? Write your answer on the line.

The first paragraph is about _____ animals.

The second one talks about _____ animals.

Wild Flowers

Count the flowers in the picture. Color one box for each color.

Flower Graph

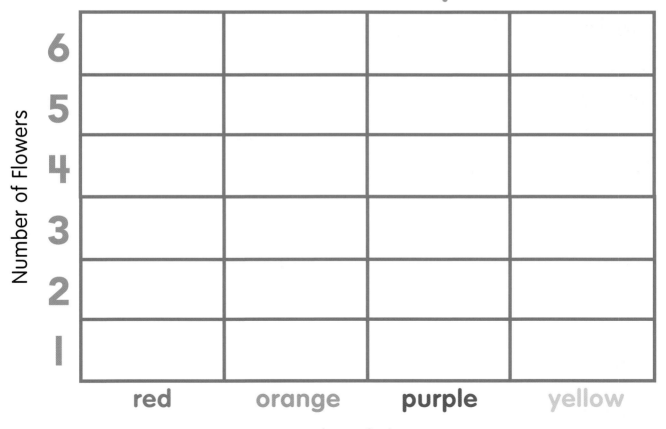

Number of Flowers

6				
5				
4				
3				
2				
1				

red   orange   **purple**   yellow

Color of Flower

Creeping By

Draw the next picture in the pattern.

Time for Consonants

Say the name for each picture. Which letter is missing from the word? Fill in the correct circle. Then, write the letter on the line.

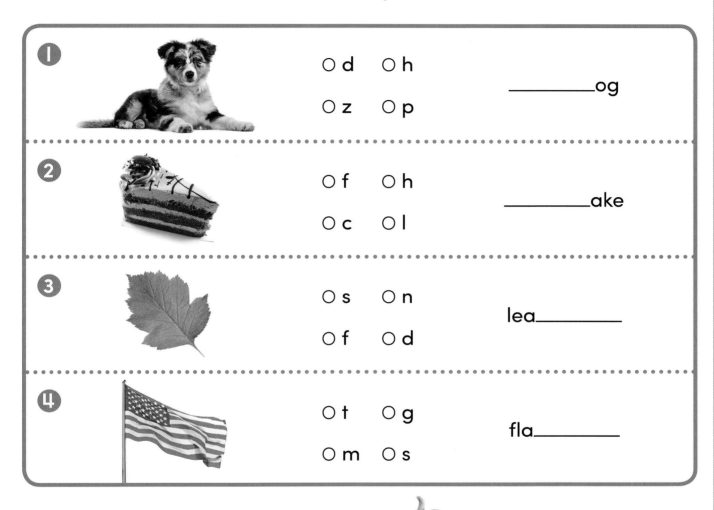

1 ○ d ○ h ○ z ○ p

_____og

2 ○ f ○ h ○ c ○ l

_____ake

3 ○ s ○ n ○ f ○ d

lea_____

4 ○ t ○ g ○ m ○ s

fla_____

Say the name for each picture. Circle if the name begins with an *s*. Circle  if it does not begin with an *s*.

From Caterpillar to Butterfly

Read the poem about butterflies. Then answer the questions.

Watch me wiggle
from my egg
leg by leg, by leg, by leg.

Watch me munch leaves high and low
and grow, and grow, and grow, and grow.

Watch the chrysalis I create
and wait, and wait, and wait, and wait.

Watch me spread new wings to dry
and fly, and fly, and fly . . . goodbye!

1 Which picture does the first sentence describe? Point to it.

2 What does the caterpillar create after it grows? Point to it.

3 What are the steps from caterpillar to butterfly? Write I, 2, or 3 below the picture that shows a step described in the poem.

What Size Am I?

In each group, circle the animal that is bigger.

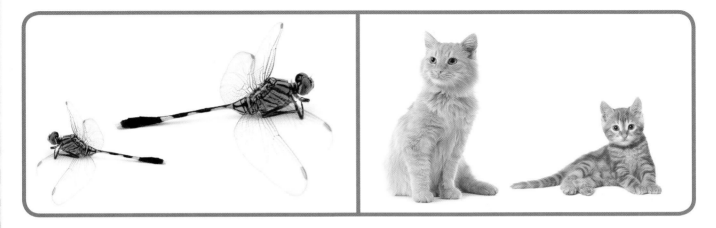

In each group, circle the tree that is taller.

In each group, circle the snake that is longer.

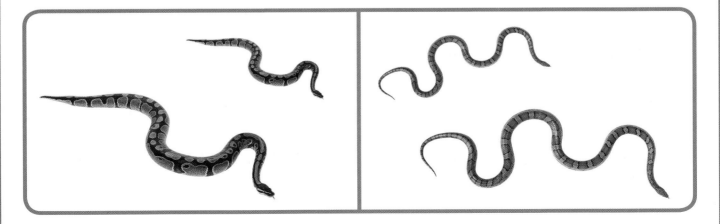

Table of Numbers

Fill in the missing numbers.

1	2		4	5		7	8	9	10
11	12	13	14	15	16	17	18		20
21		23	24		26	27	28	29	
31	32	33		35	36	37		39	40
	42	43	44	45	46		48	49	50
51	52		54	55	56	57	58	59	
61		63	64	65	66		68	69	70
	72	73	74		76	77	78	79	80
81	82	83	84		86	87		89	90

116

Help Your Child Get Ready: Week 10

Here are some activities that you and your child might enjoy.

Sight Word Search

While flipping through a magazine, encourage your child to look for sight words such as *the, of, to, you, she, my, is, are, do,* and *does.* Have your child say and circle the words. Then have your child count how many of each word they found on a page or in an article.

Making Words

On a small chalkboard or whiteboard, write new words with phonograms. For example, starting with the word *cat,* erase the *c* and encourage your child to write a different consonant in its place to make a new word, such as *hat, bat,* or *mat.* Make sure all the words used are real.

Stargazing

Take your child out on a clear, dark night to gaze at the stars. Point out familiar constellations, such as Orion or the Big Dipper. Then, encourage your child to "connect the stars" to create and name his or her own patterns.

Counting Coins

Give your child a collection of different coins. Ask your child to find different ways of making 50 cents or $1.

These are the skills your child will be working on this week.

Math
- skip count by 2s, 5s, and 10s
- identify patterns
- draw shapes
- addition within 20
- number sequence through 100

Foundational Skills
- spelling
- understand antonyms

Reading
- identify key details

Phonics
- high-frequency word *do*
- understand letter-sound correspondences
- beginning and ending consonants
- short vowels

Incentive Chart: Week 10

Week 10	Day 1	Day 2	Day 3	Day 4	Day 5
Put a sticker to show you completed each day's work.	☆ ☆	☆ ☆	☆ ☆	☆ ☆	☆ ☆

CONGRATULATIONS!

Wow! You did a great job this week!

This certificate is presented to:

_____

_____   _____
Date   Parent/Caregiver's Signature

Sight Word: *do*

Trace and write *do* on the line.

Find each hippo that has *do*. Trace its path to the water

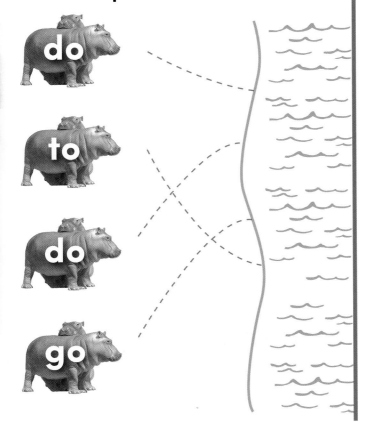

Write the missing letters to spell *do*.

d ___

___ ___ o

Circle each pair of flowers that has *do*.

Lost and Found

What's in the lost and found? Say the name for each picture. Circle the letter that completes each word. Write it in the blank.

l   k   m

boo_____

h   c   t

boo_____

c   p   n

_____en

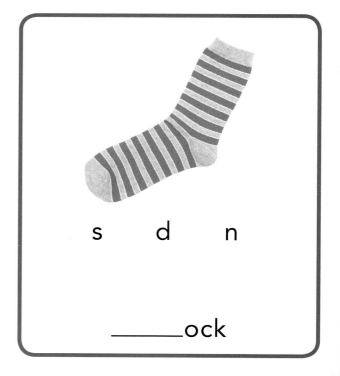

s   d   n

_____ock

Jars of Jam

Skip-count the jars. Write the missing numbers.

Count by 2s.

6   8   __   __   14   16   __

Count by 5s.

15   20   __   30   __   __   45

Count by 10s.

30   __   50   60   __   __   90

Patterns

Finish labeling each pattern.

1 __A__ __A__ __B__ __A__ __A__ __B__ _____ _____ _____

2 __A__ __A__ __B__ __A__ _____ _____ _____ _____ _____

Draw your own AAB pattern. Use pictures.

_____ _____ _____ _____ _____ _____
A   A   B   A   A   B

Missing Letters

Add a letter to complete the name of the object in each picture.

do_____

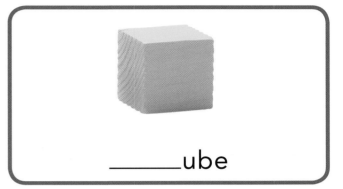

_____ube

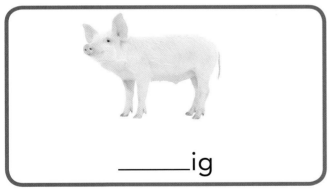

b_____ ke

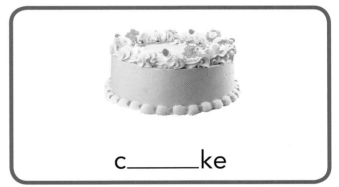

c_____ke

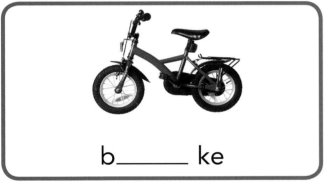

_____ig

ca_____

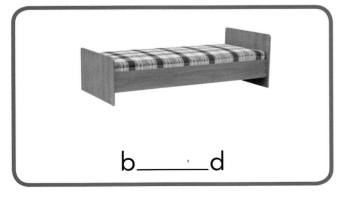

b_____d

_____ose

Matching Opposites

Read each word. Then draw a line to match words that are opposites. Use the pictures to help.

big

night

day

sad

long

small

happy

short

Shapely Addition Once More

Review shapes.

Draw three circles. | Draw four squares.

Use the number line to solve each problem.

| 1 | 2 | 3 | 4 | 5 | 6 | 7 | 8 | 9 | 10 |

| 11 | 12 | 13 | 14 | 15 | 16 | 17 | 18 | 19 | 20 |

1
$$10$$
$$+\,5$$

2
$$10$$
$$+\,10$$

3
$$11$$
$$+\,7$$

4
$$13$$
$$+\,6$$

5
$$11$$
$$+\,9$$

6
$$9$$
$$+\,8$$

How Many Leaves?

Count the objects in each set. Write the number in the box.

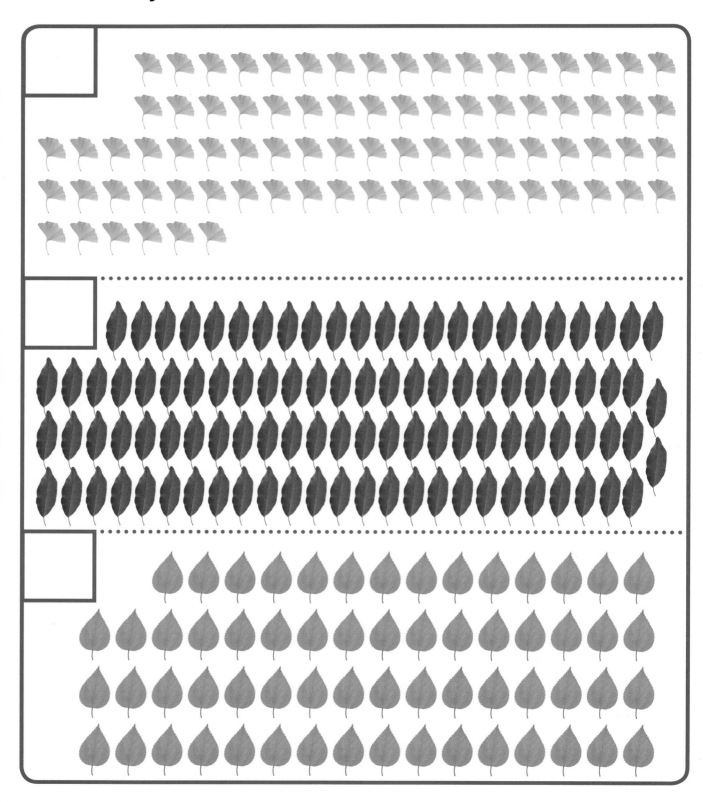

Missing Vowels

Add a vowel to each puzzle to make two words.
Use the pictures as clues.

p
d   g
t

m
c   t
p

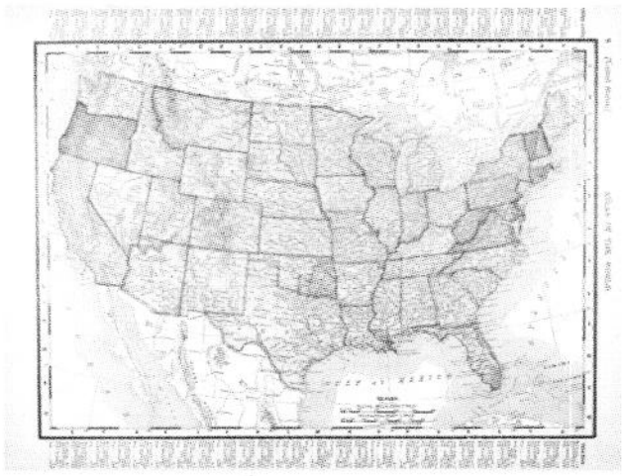

b
w   b
d

p
b   b
g

j
c   p
g

A Noise

Read the story. Then, answer the questions.

Li and Aya were walking home.
They passed a tall tree.

The girls heard a spooky noise.
Was it crying? They stopped walking.
They held hands.

Then Aya smiled and pointed up.
"Look!" she said.

Li saw the kitten. "Oh, kitty!"
said Li. "We will get help for you."

❶ Why did the girls hold hands?
○ to cross a street
○ Li was crying
○ to feel safer

❷ What made the noise? _____

_____

_____

Answer Key

Week 1

Letter Friends

Help these letters find their friends. Draw a line to match each uppercase letter with its lowercase letter.

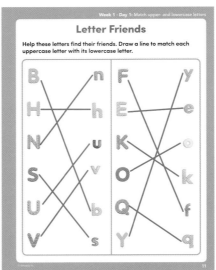

Letter Friends

Help these letters find their friends. Draw a line to match each uppercase letter with its lowercase letter.

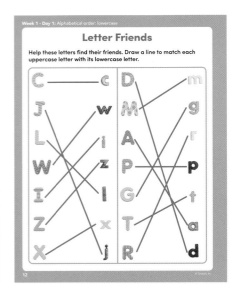

Count Across Our Country

Count. Then write the number on the line.

There are **4** seashells on the beach.

There are **4** bison on the plain.

There are **3** cacti in the desert.

There are **5** trees in the prairie.

What's the Missing Number?

Some of the number blocks are missing numbers! Fill in the missing numbers. Then print the numbers one to ten below.

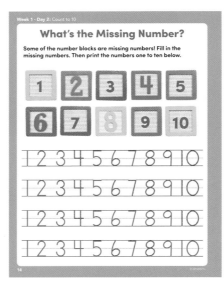

Match Me!

Draw a line from each picture to its beginning sound.

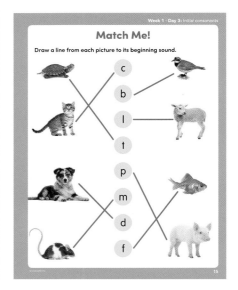

Fill-In Rhymes

Rhyming words sound alike. Read the rhyme. Circle the rhyming pictures to finish the poem.

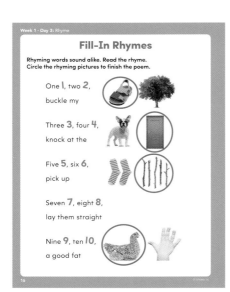

One 1, two 2, buckle my

Three 3, four 4, knock at the

Five 5, six 6, pick up

Seven 7, eight 8, lay them straight

Nine 9, ten 10, a good fat

What's the Scoop?

Count the scoops on each ice cream cone. Write the number on the cone.

1. Circle the cone with the fewest scoops.
2. Put an ✗ on two cones with an equal number of scoops.
3. Put a ✔ on the cone with the most chocolate scoops.
4. How many scoops of ice cream are there in total? **20**

How Many Fish?

Count the fish in each bowl. Write the number in the box. Then, in each set, circle the bowl that has more.

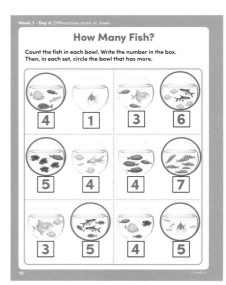

Short-*a* Words

Some words have the short-*a* sound, like *cat*.
Look at the pictures. Say the words. Listen to the short-*a* sound.
Underline the short *a* in each word.

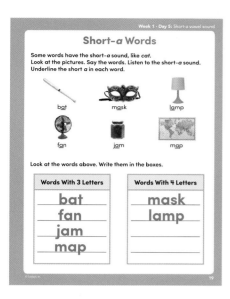

bat   mask   lamp
fan   jam   map

Look at the words above. Write them in the boxes.

Words With 3 Letters	Words With 4 Letters
bat	mask
fan	lamp
jam	
map	

A Snack for the Cats

The cats like snacks with the short-*a* sound. Look at the pictures
in each box. Say the words. Listen for the short-*a* sound.
Circle the snacks each cat likes best.

Week 2

Sight Word: *the*

Trace and write *the* on the line.

Find each leaf that has *the*.
Trace the path from that
leaf to the basket.

Write the missing letters
to spell *the*.

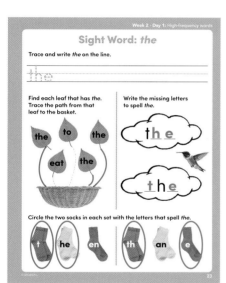

Circle the two socks in each set with the letters that spell *the*.

Rhyme Time!

Write a letter in the blank space to make a rhyming pair.

Marble Match

Draw a line to match each number to its number word.

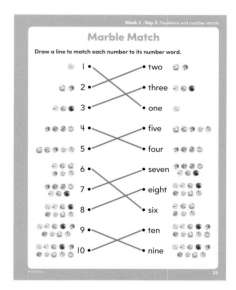

1	two
2	three
3	one
4	five
5	four
6	seven
7	eight
8	six
9	ten
10	nine

Count the Sleeping Animals!

Count the animals. Write the number and the number word.

Number Key					
1	2	3	4	5	6
one	two	three	four	five	six

2 two
4 four
5 five
1 one

Short-*e* Words

Some words have the short-*e* sound like *ten*.
Look at the pictures. Say the words. Listen to the short-*e* sound.
Underline the short *e* in each word.

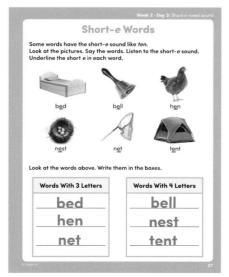

bed   bell   hen
nest   net   tent

Look at the words above. Write them in the boxes.

Words With 3 Letters	Words With 4 Letters
bed	bell
hen	nest
net	tent

Hen's Nest

Hen likes the short-*e* sound. Say the names
for the pictures in each box. Listen for the
short-*e* sound. Circle the short-*e* pictures.

131

The Best Nest

Read the poem.
Underline all the words that end with -est.

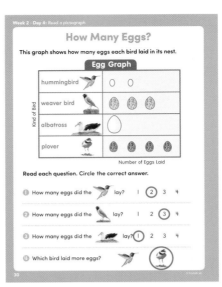

If you see a robin's nest,
It is best to let it rest.
Do not ever be a pest,
Just let that bird's nest rest!

Look at Robin in her nest,
Folded wings across her chest.
She protects her eggs the best,
In her little nest.

Peck—an eggshell gets a test.
One egg's hatching before the rest.
CRACK! It's open! That's the best—
A new chick's in the nest!

29

How Many Eggs?

This graph shows how many eggs each bird laid in its nest.

Egg Graph

Read each question. Circle the correct answer.

① How many eggs did the [bird] lay?   1   (2)   3   4

② How many eggs did the [bird] lay?   1   2   (3)   4

③ How many eggs did the [bird] lay?   (1)   2   3   4

④ Which bird laid more eggs? [bird]   (bird)

30

You Can Count on Me!

Count. Then fill in the blanks.

Check your child's work.

① I have ☐ letters in my name.

② I am ☐ years old.

③ There are ☐ [people] in my home.
people

④ There are ☐ [windows] in my home.
windows

⑤ There are ☐ [chairs] in my home.
chairs

31

I Can Count to 15!

Write the missing numbers.

9, 10, 11, 12, __13__, 14, __15__

Count the number of objects in each box and circle that number.

(15)   14   11   12   14   (13)   (11)   14   13

Apples sometimes fall from trees.
Draw 15 apples on the ground.

Check your child's work.

32

Week 3

Number Pattern

Write the numbers to complete each pattern.

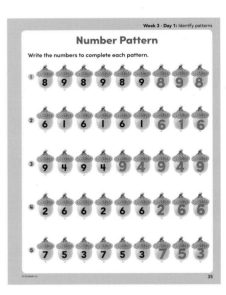

① 8 9 8 9 8 9 8 9 8 9 8

② 6 1 6 1 6 1 6 1 6

③ 9 4 9 4 9 4 9 4 9

④ 2 6 6 2 6 6 2 6 2 6 6

⑤ 7 5 3 7 5 3 7 5 3

35

How Many More Make 5?

Draw more eggs so that each nest has 5.
Then finish the number sentence.

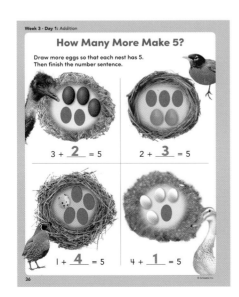

3 + __2__ = 5   2 + __3__ = 5

1 + __4__ = 5   4 + __1__ = 5

36

Sight Word: of

Trace and write of on the line.

Draw a line from each duck to the puddle that has of.   Write of on each duck.

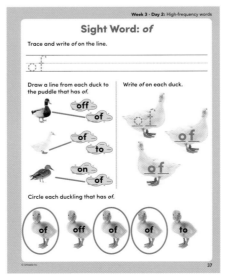

Circle each duckling that has of.

of   off   of   of   to

37

Off the Log

Read. Then write the names of the frogs in the picture.

Two frogs sit on a log.

"I will hop off," says one.

"I will swim off," says the other.

Hank hops. Suzy swims.

Who is Hank? Who is Suzy?

Hank

Suzy

38

Tentacles and Legs

Finish the ocean animals.
Then complete each number sentence.

Draw tentacles so each jellyfish has 5.

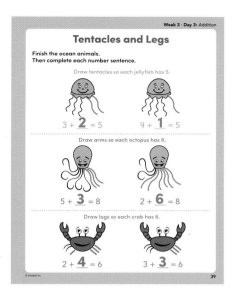

$3 + \mathbf{2} = 5$ $4 + \mathbf{1} = 5$

Draw arms so each octopus has 8.

$5 + \mathbf{3} = 8$ $2 + \mathbf{6} = 8$

Draw legs so each crab has 6.

$2 + \mathbf{4} = 6$ $3 + \mathbf{3} = 6$

39

Count the Objects

Count the correct number of objects.
Draw an X through the extra objects.

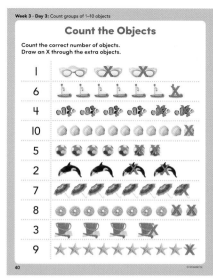

1
6
4
10
5
2
7
8
3
9

40

Short-*i* Words

Some words have the short-*i* sound like *six*.
Say the name for each picture. Listen to the short-*i* sound.
Underline the short *i* in each word.

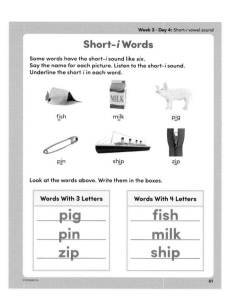

fish   milk   pig

pin   ship   zip

Look at the words above. Write them in the boxes.

Words With 3 Letters	Words With 4 Letters
pig	fish
pin	milk
zip	ship

41

Pig's Picture

Pig takes pictures of the short-*i* sound.
Say the name for each picture. Listen
for the short-*i* sound. Circle the word,
then write it.

fox (fish)
fish

show (ship)
ship

soap (sink)
sink

(milk) make
milk

42

Counting Windows

Write the missing numbers.

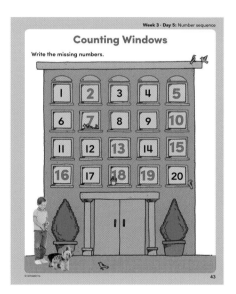

1 2 3 4 5
6 7 8 9 10
11 12 13 14 15
16 17 18 19 20

43

I Can Count to 20!

Write the missing numbers.

15, 16, __17__, __18__, 19, __20__

Count the number of objects in each box and circle that number.

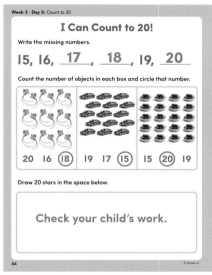

20 16 (18)   19 17 (15)   15 (20) 19

Draw 20 stars in the space below.

Check your child's work.

44

Week 4

Sight Word: *to*

Trace and write *to* on the line.

to

Find each coin that has *to*.
Trace the path from that coin
to the bank.

Write *to* on each tent.

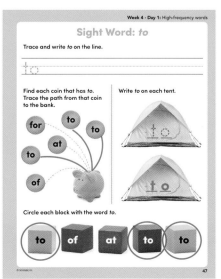

for
to
at
to
of

to
to

Circle each block with the word *to*.

(to) of at (to) (to)

47

Rhyme Time!

Choose a letter from the box to complete each rhyming pair.

h g c b w p

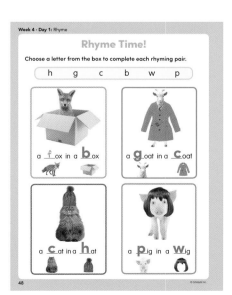

a **f**ox in a **b**ox   a **g**oat in a **c**oat

a **c**at in a **h**at   a **p**ig in a **w**ig

48

Red, White, and Blue!

Count the objects in each group. Then write the number in the box below. Finally, circle the group that has more.

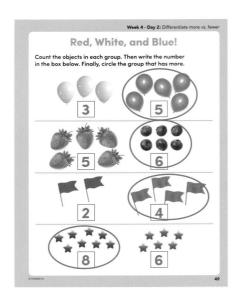

Let's Count

Count the correct number of objects.
Draw an X through the extra objects.

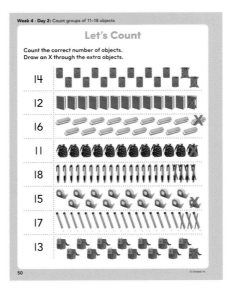

14
12
16
11
18
15
17
13

Ants Came to Our Picnic!

What did they carry away?
Choose a letter from the box to complete each word.

| p | a | w | i | b | f | c | ch |

f ork   a pple   p izza

c orn   b anana   w atermelon

i ce cream   **Challenge:** ch eese

Wally the Whale

Read the story. Then read each sentence.
Is the sentence true or false? X the correct box.

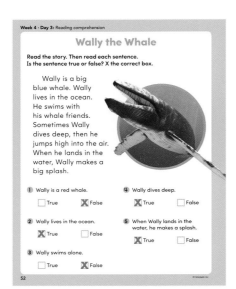

Wally is a big blue whale. Wally lives in the ocean. He swims with his whale friends. Sometimes Wally dives deep, then he jumps high into the air. When he lands in the water, Wally makes a big splash.

1 Wally is a red whale.
☐ True   ☒ False

2 Wally lives in the ocean.
☒ True   ☐ False

3 Wally swims alone.
☐ True   ☒ False

4 Wally dives deep.
☒ True   ☐ False

5 When Wally lands in the water, he makes a splash.
☒ True   ☐ False

Back From the Beach

Write the answer for each problem.
Then use the code to answer the question.

n $7 - 2 =$ **5**   e $6 - 3 =$ **3**   r $8 - 1 =$ **7**

i $8 - 0 =$ **8**   m $7 - 1 =$ **6**   d $8 - 4 =$ **4**

f $5 - 3 =$ **2**   o $8 - 8 =$ **0**   t $3 - 2 =$ **1**

What will you hear when you walk into the house?

Use the code to find out.

t i m e   f o r
1 8 6 3   2 0 7

d i n n e r !
4 8 5 5 3 7

A Race to the Finish Line

Help Charlie and Jennifer reach the finish line.
Fill in the missing numbers along the path.

Short-o Words

Some words have the short-o sound like *sock*.
Say the name for each picture. Listen to the short-o sound.
Underline the short o in each word.

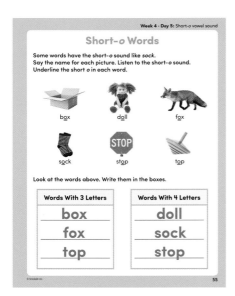

box   doll   fox

sock   stop   top

Look at the words above. Write them in the boxes.

Words With 3 Letters	Words With 4 Letters
box	doll
fox	sock
top	stop

A Toy Box for Fox

Fox's favorite toys have the short-o sound. Look at the pictures. Say the words. Listen for the short-o sound. Circle the word, then write it.

boat (block)   **block**

(frog) flag   **frog**

tent (top)   **top**

(doll) duck   **doll**

Week 5

49
50
51
52
53
54
55
56

134

Summer Skip Counting

1. Count the bikes' wheels by 2s. There are **8** wheels in all.

2. Count the paddles by 2s. There are **6** paddles in all.

3. Count the ears by 2s. There are **10** ears in all.

4. Count the flip flops by 2s. There are **10** flip flops in all.

59

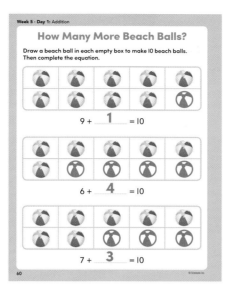

How Many More Beach Balls?

Draw a beach ball in each empty box to make 10 beach balls. Then complete the equation.

$9 + \mathbf{1} = 10$

$6 + \mathbf{4} = 10$

$7 + \mathbf{3} = 10$

60

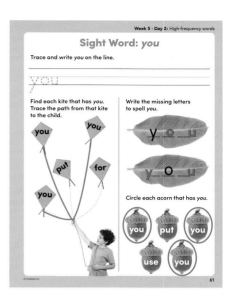

Sight Word: *you*

Trace and write *you* on the line.

you

Find each kite that has *you*. Trace the path from that kite to the child.

you   you   put   for   you

Write the missing letters to spell *you*.

y _ o _ u

y _ o _ u

Circle each acorn that has *you*.

you   put   you
use   you

61

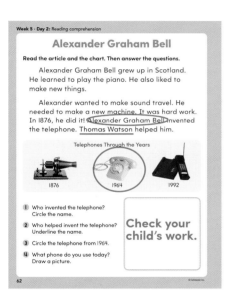

Alexander Graham Bell

Read the article and the chart. Then answer the questions.

Alexander Graham Bell grew up in Scotland. He learned to play the piano. He also liked to make new things.

Alexander wanted to make sound travel. He needed to make a new machine. It was hard work. In 1876, he did it! Alexander Graham Bell invented the telephone. Thomas Watson helped him.

Telephones Through the Years

1876   1964   1992

1. Who invented the telephone? Circle the name.
2. Who helped invent the telephone? Underline the name.
3. Circle the telephone from 1964.
4. What phone do you use today? Draw a picture.

Check your child's work.

62

An Ocean Code

First, solve these math problems.

$\begin{array}{c} 2 \\ +3 \\ \hline \mathbf{5} \end{array}$ $\begin{array}{c} 2 \\ +1 \\ \hline \mathbf{3} \end{array}$ $\begin{array}{c} 6 \\ +1 \\ \hline \mathbf{7} \end{array}$ $\begin{array}{c} 2 \\ +2 \\ \hline \mathbf{4} \end{array}$

V   W   S   A

$\begin{array}{c} 1 \\ +1 \\ \hline \mathbf{2} \end{array}$ $\begin{array}{c} 1 \\ +0 \\ \hline \mathbf{1} \end{array}$ $\begin{array}{c} 3 \\ +3 \\ \hline \mathbf{6} \end{array}$

T   I   E

Now put the letters in the correct space below. You will find the answer to a joke!

How can you tell that the ocean is friendly?

I T   W A V E S !
1 2   3 4 5 6 7

63

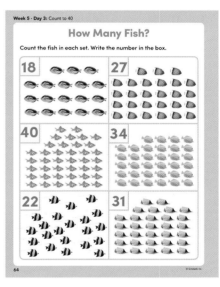

How Many Fish?

Count the fish in each set. Write the number in the box.

18   27
40   34
22   31

64

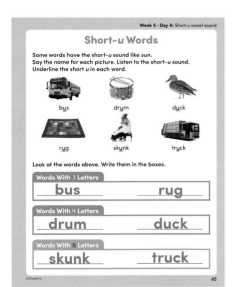

Short-*u* Words

Some words have the short-*u* sound like *sun*. Say the name for each picture. Listen to the short-*u* sound. Underline the short *u* in each word.

bus   drum   duck
rug   skunk   truck

Look at the words above. Write them in the boxes.

Words With 3 Letters
bus   rug

Words With 4 Letters
drum   duck

Words With 5 Letters
skunk   truck

65

Bug's Busy Day

Bug had a busy day! Say the name for each picture. Circle the word, then write it. Use the words to tell a story about Bug's busy day.

up   cup
up

run   bun
run

juggle   just
juggle

tub   tug
tub

66

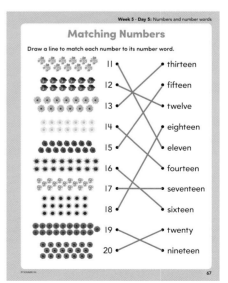

Matching Numbers

Draw a line to match each number to its number word.

11 — thirteen
12 — fifteen
13 — twelve
14 — eighteen
15 — eleven
16 — fourteen
17 — seventeen
18 — sixteen
19 — twenty
20 — nineteen

67

Big Bowl of Jellybeans

Draw 50 jellybeans inside the bowl. Use the colors shown.
Then answer the question below.

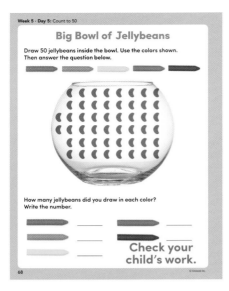

How many jellybeans did you draw in each color?
Write the number.

Check your
child's work.

68

Week 6

Sight Word: *she*

Trace and write *she* on the line.

she

Trace each flower that has *she*.

Write the missing letters to spell *she*.

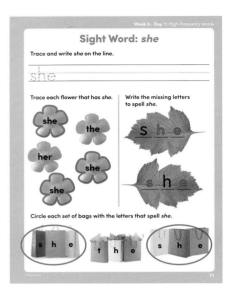

she | the | her | she | she

s h e
s h e

Circle each set of bags with the letters that spell *she*.

s h e | the | s h e

71

Lunch Buddies

Read the story, then answer the questions.

Roger was feeling a little sad. It was the first day of school, and he had no one to eat lunch with. Roger saw a new boy who looked sad, too.

"Is something wrong?" Roger asked.

"I forgot to bring my lunch money," said the boy.

"I have a big lunch," said Roger, "Why don't you sit with me? Then we can share."

1. This story is mostly about
   ○ forgetting lunch.
   ○ feeling hungry.
   ● finding a lunch buddy.

2. Where does this story take place?
   ● at school
   ○ at Roger's home
   ○ on the playground

3. What do you think will happen the next day?
   ○ The new boy will forget his money.
   ● The boys will sit together.
   ○ The boys will both feel sad.

72

What Shape Am I?

Draw a line from each picture to its matching shape.

square
oval
diamond
rectangle
triangle
circle

73

Take It Away

Solve each problem. Cross out objects to help you subtract.
Write each answer.

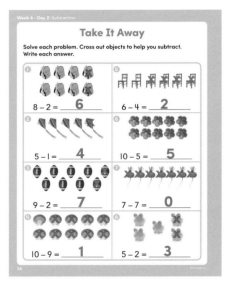

1. $8 - 2 = 6$
2. $5 - 1 = 4$
3. $9 - 2 = 7$
4. $10 - 9 = 1$
5. $6 - 4 = 2$
6. $10 - 5 = 5$
7. $7 - 7 = 0$
8. $5 - 2 = 3$

74

Match My Sounds!

Draw a line from each picture to its ending sounds.

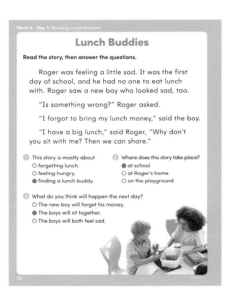

g
r
m
p
t
n
d
x

75

One Word Out

Some words belong together
Because they are alike.
Words like *seat*, *wheels*, and *pedals*
Are all part of my bike.

Big, *large*, and *huge*
Are words that mean the same.
Tag, *jump rope*, and *hopscotch*
Are all kinds of fun games.

Let's see if you can choose
The word that does not fit
In each group of words below:
Just find and circle it!

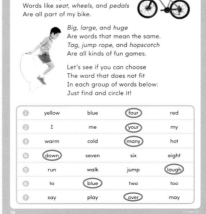

1	yellow	blue	(four)	red
2	I	me	(your)	my
3	warm	cold	(many)	hot
4	(down)	seven	six	eight
5	run	walk	jump	(laugh)
6	to	(blue)	two	too
7	say	play	(over)	may

76

Graph the Garden

Look at the garden.
Color one box in the graph for each item you see.

Garden Graph

Garden Item				
carrot				4
worm		2	3	4
ladybug			3	4
flower				

Number of Items

77

How Many Are There?

Count the objects in each set. Write the number in the box.

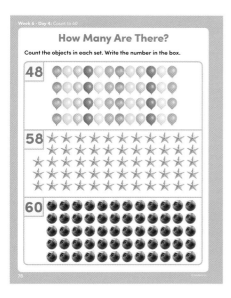

48	
58	
60	

Silent-e Words

A vowel can sound like its name. This is called a long-vowel sound. Look at the pictures. Say the words. Listen for the sound of *a* and *i*. Underline *a* and *i*.

bike   cake   gate

kite   mice   rake

Look at the words above. Write them in the boxes.

Words With Long *a*	Words With Long *i*
cake	bike
gate	kite
rake	mice

Long or Short?

Circle each picture with a long-vowel sound.

nine	hat	lake
snake	rice	log
wig	cape	crab

Add a letter to complete the name of each object.

c__a__ke   b__i__ke

Week 7

Fewer or More

Fill in the blank to make the sentence true. Use *fewer* or *more*.

24 teeth   34 teeth

0 teeth   80 teeth

① An elephant has **more** teeth than a turtle.

② A camel has **fewer** teeth than an alligator.

30 teeth   42 teeth   98 teeth   36 teeth

③ A cat has **fewer** teeth than a dog.

④ A dolphin has **more** teeth than a hippo.

Math Problem of the Day

Use the cups to solve each problem.

$9 - \underline{4} = 5$ $6 - \underline{1} = 5$

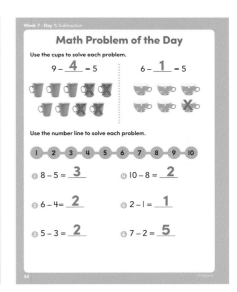

Use the number line to solve each problem.

1 2 3 4 5 6 7 8 9 10

① $8 - 5 = \underline{3}$ ④ $10 - 8 = \underline{2}$

② $6 - 4 = \underline{2}$ ⑤ $2 - 1 = \underline{1}$

③ $5 - 3 = \underline{2}$ ⑥ $7 - 2 = \underline{5}$

Sight Word: *my*

Trace and write *my* on the line.

my

Circle each section that has *my*.

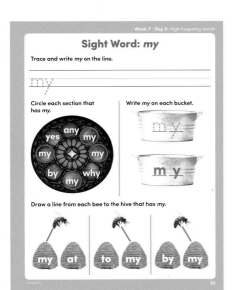

yes any my
my   my
by   why
my

Write *my* on each bucket.

my

my

Draw a line from each bee to the hive that has *my*.

my at   to my   by my

Snakes Are Everywhere!

Read the article. Then answer the questions.

Some snakes live in forests. Some live in hot, dry deserts. Others live in lakes or streams. Some snakes even live in the sea! Snakes live almost everywhere. But they never live where it is always freezing cold.

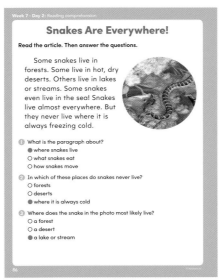

① What is the paragraph about?
   ● where snakes live
   ○ what snakes eat
   ○ how snakes move

② In which of these places do snakes never live?
   ○ forests
   ○ deserts
   ● where it is always cold

③ Where does the snake in the photo most likely live?
   ○ a forest
   ○ a desert
   ● a lake or stream

Word Problems

Draw a picture to solve each problem. Write the number sentence on the line.

① Lori picked up four acorns. Then she picked up three more acorns. How many acorns does Lori have?

$4 + 3 = 7$

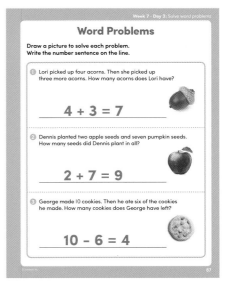

② Dennis planted two apple seeds and seven pumpkin seeds. How many seeds did Dennis plant in all?

$2 + 7 = 9$

③ George made 10 cookies. Then he ate six of the cookies he made. How many cookies does George have left?

$10 - 6 = 4$

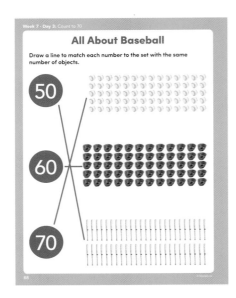

All About Baseball

Draw a line to match each number to the set with the same number of objects.

50
60
70

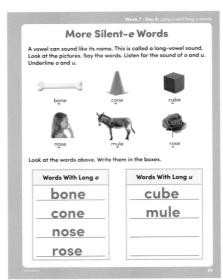

More Silent-*e* Words

A vowel can sound like its name. This is called a long-vowel sound. Look at the pictures. Say the words. Listen for the sound of *o* and *u*. Underline *o* and *u*.

bone   cone   cube

nose   mule   rose

Look at the words above. Write them in the boxes.

Words With Long *o*	Words With Long *u*
bone	cube
cone	mule
nose	
rose	

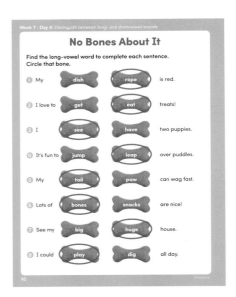

No Bones About It

Find the long-vowel word to complete each sentence. Circle that bone.

1. My **dish** / **rope** is red.
2. I love to **get** / **eat** treats!
3. I **see** / **have** two puppies.
4. It's fun to **jump** / **leap** over puddles.
5. My **tail** / **paw** can wag fast.
6. Lots of **bones** / **snacks** are nice!
7. See my **big** / **huge** house.
8. I could **play** / **dig** all day.

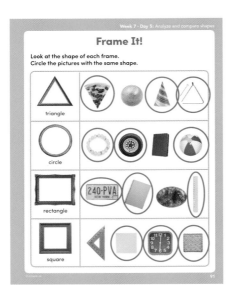

Frame It!

Look at the shape of each frame. Circle the pictures with the same shape.

triangle

circle

rectangle

square

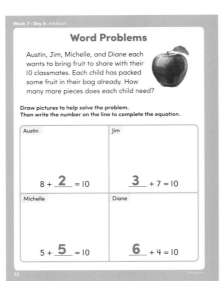

Word Problems

Austin, Jim, Michelle, and Diane each wants to bring fruit to share with their 10 classmates. Each child has packed some fruit in their bag already. How many more pieces does each child need?

Draw pictures to help solve the problem. Then write the number on the line to complete the equation.

Austin	Jim
8 + **2** = 10	**3** + 7 = 10
Michelle	Diane
5 + **5** = 10	**6** + 4 = 10

Week 8

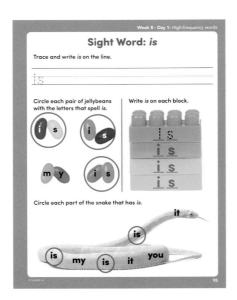

Sight Word: *is*

Trace and write *is* on the line.

is

Circle each pair of jellybeans with the letters that spell *is*.

i s   i s
m y   i s

Write *is* on each block.

i s
i s
i s
i s

Circle each part of the snake that has *is*.

it
is
is my is it you

The Forgotten Panda

Read the story. Then answer the questions.

Each morning Gail walks Carol, her little sister, to school. She holds Carol's hand. Gail makes sure Carol gets to her classroom safely. Today Carol is crying. She is **upset**. Why? Carol forgot her panda for show-and-tell. Gail cannot get her sister to stop crying.

1. What will most likely happen next?
   ○ Gail will send Carol home to get the panda.
   ○ Gail will leave Carol on the sidewalk crying.
   ● Gail will take Carol home to get the panda.

2. What can you tell about Gail from this story?
   ● Gail is a good sister.
   ○ Gail forgot Carol.
   ○ Gail forgot the panda.

3. In this story, what does the word **upset** mean?
   ○ knock over
   ● unhappy
   ○ upside down

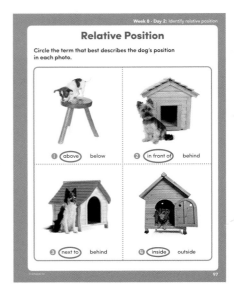

Relative Position

Circle the term that best describes the dog's position in each photo.

1. **above** / below
2. **in front of** / behind
3. **next to** / behind
4. **inside** / outside

Shapely Addition

Review shapes.

Draw three ovals.

Draw two rectangles.

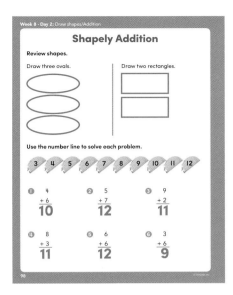

Use the number line to solve each problem.

3 4 5 6 7 8 9 10 11 12

❶ 4
+ 6
10

❷ 5
+ 7
12

❸ 9
+ 2
11

❹ 8
+ 3
11

❺ 6
+ 6
12

❻ 3
+ 6
9

98

I Spy Animals

Play "I Spy Animals." Say the name of the animals in each box. Clap and count the syllables for each. Circle the animal that matches the number of syllables listed in each box.

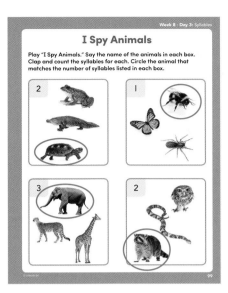

99

Begin and End With Consonants

Read the letter in each row. Fill in the circle next to each picture whose name begins with that sound.

❶ n

❷ d

❸ f

Read the letter in each row. Fill in the circle next to each picture whose name ends with that sound.

❹ k

❺ s

❻ t

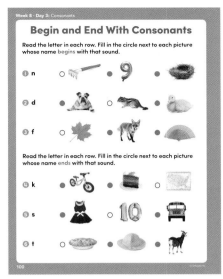

100

Count the Cookies

Look at the number on each jar. Count the cookies in each set. Draw a line to match the cookies to the jar with the same number.

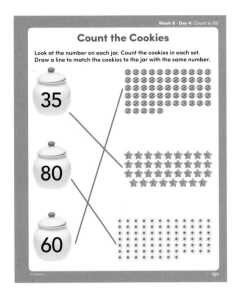

35

80

60

101

More Shapely Addition

Review shapes.

Draw five squares.

Draw four triangles.

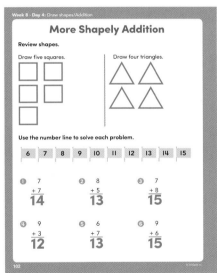

Use the number line to solve each problem.

6 7 8 9 10 11 12 13 14 15

❶ 7
+ 7
14

❷ 8
+ 5
13

❸ 7
+ 8
15

❹ 9
+ 3
12

❺ 6
+ 7
13

❻ 9
+ 6
15

102

Animal Facts

Write s on the lines. Then, read the sentences.

Zebra**s** have lot**s** of stripe**s**.

Frog**s** eat lot**s** of bug**s**.

Leopard**s** have lot**s** of spot**s**.

And teddy bear**s** give hug**s**!

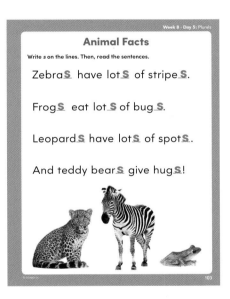

103

Fun Phonics

Circle the word that names each picture.

❶ (door) / deer / dare

❷ shape / sharp / (sheep)

❸ (seeds) / said / sand

❹ keen / seen / (queen)

❺ foot / (feet) / felt

❻ (wheel) / where / week

Color Words

Trace. Then write.

red

pink

green

yellow

104

Week 9

Seed Graph

Read the graph. Then circle the correct answers.

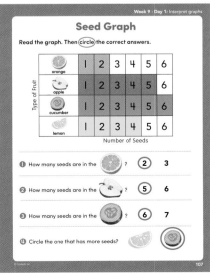

Type of Fruit						
orange	1	2	3	4	5	6
apple	1	2	3	4	5	6
cucumber	1	2	3	4	5	6
lemon	1	2	3	4	5	6

Number of Seeds

❶ How many seeds are in the ? (2) 3

❷ How many seeds are in the ? (5) 6

❸ How many seeds are in the ? (6) 7

❹ Circle the one that has more seeds?

107

139

Blast Off

Add or subtract. Then use the code to answer the riddle below.

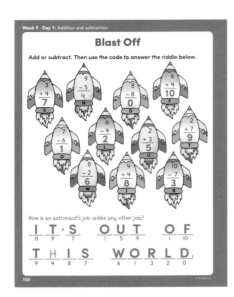

$3 + 4 = 7$ S
$9 - 5 = 4$ H
$9 - 8 = D$ ... $+ 10$ F
$7 - 6 = 1$ O
$6 - 2 = L$ ... $+ 3 = 5$ U ... $2 + 7 = 9$ T
$8 - 6 = W$ ... $4 + 8 = I$ ... $10 - 7 = R$

How is an astronaut's job unlike any other job?

I T ' S   O U T   O F
8 9 7   1 5 9   1 0

T H I S   W O R L D
9 4 8 7   6 1 3 2 0

108

Sight Word: *are*

Trace and write *are* on the line.

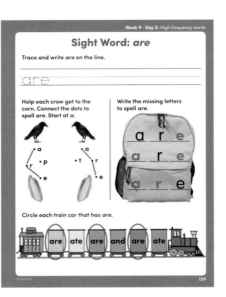

Help each crow get to the corn. Connect the dots to spell *are*. Start at *a*.

Write the missing letters to spell *are*.

are
are
are

Circle each train car that has *are*.

are   ate   are   and   are   ate

109

Whales and Elephants

Animals are amazing! Read each paragraph. Answer the questions.

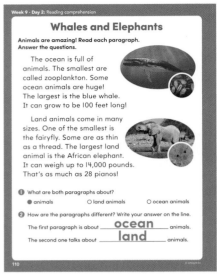

The ocean is full of animals. The smallest are called zooplankton. Some ocean animals are huge! The largest is the blue whale. It can grow to be 100 feet long!

Land animals come in many sizes. One of the smallest is the fairyfly. Some are as thin as a thread. The largest land animal is the African elephant. It can weigh up to 14,000 pounds. That's as much as 28 pianos!

1. What are both paragraphs about?
   ● animals   ○ land animals   ○ ocean animals

2. How are the paragraphs different? Write your answer on the line.
   The first paragraph is about **ocean** animals.
   The second one talks about **land** animals.

110

Wild Flowers

Count the flowers in the picture. Color one box for each color.

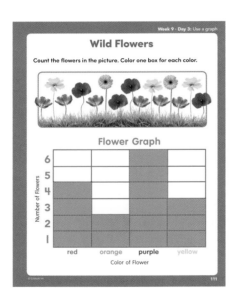

Flower Graph

Number of Flowers	red	orange	purple	yellow
6			■	
5			■	
4	■		■	
3	■		■	■
2	■	■	■	■
1	■	■	■	■

Color of Flower

111

Creeping By

Draw the next picture in the pattern.

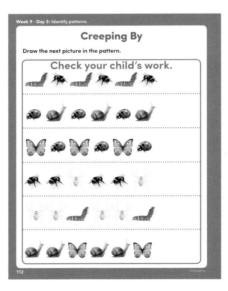

Check your child's work.

112

Time for Consonants

Say the name for each picture. Which letter is missing from the word? Fill in the correct circle. Then, write the letter on the line.

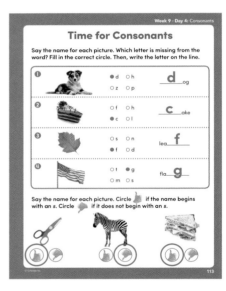

1. ○ d   ○ h   ○ z   ○ p   **d** og
2. ○ f   ○ h   ● c   ○ l   **c** ake
3. ○ s   ○ n   ● f   ○ d   lea **f**
4. ○ t   ● g   ○ m   ○ s   fla **g**

Say the name for each picture. Circle 👍 if the name begins with an *s*. Circle 👎 if it does not begin with an *s*.

113

From Caterpillar to Butterfly

Read the poem about butterflies. Then answer the questions.

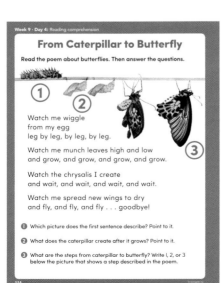

Watch me wiggle
from my egg
leg by leg, by leg.

Watch me munch leaves high and low
and grow, and grow, and grow, and grow.

Watch the chrysalis I create
and wait, and wait, and wait, and wait.

Watch me spread new wings to dry
and fly, and fly, and fly . . . goodbye!

1. Which picture does the first sentence describe? Point to it.

2. What does the caterpillar create after it grows? Point to it.

3. What are the steps from caterpillar to butterfly? Write 1, 2, or 3 below the picture that shows a step described in the poem.

114

What Size Am I?

In each group, circle the animal that is bigger.

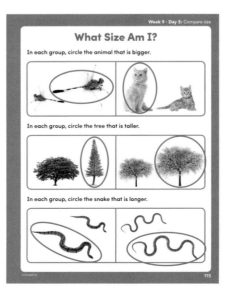

In each group, circle the tree that is taller.

In each group, circle the snake that is longer.

115

Table of Numbers

Fill in the missing numbers.

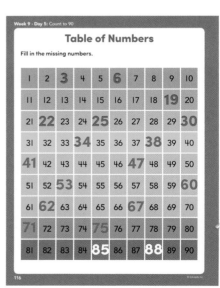

1	2	3	4	5	6	7	8	9	10
11	12	13	14	15	16	17	18	19	20
21	22	23	24	25	26	27	28	29	30
31	32	33	34	35	36	37	38	39	40
41	42	43	44	45	46	47	48	49	50
51	52	53	54	55	56	57	58	59	60
61	62	63	64	65	66	67	68	69	70
71	72	73	74	75	76	77	78	79	80
81	82	83	84	85	86	87	88	89	90

116

Week 10

Sight Word: *do*

Trace and write *do* on the line.

Find each hippo that has *do*. Trace its path to the water

do
to
do
go

Write the missing letters to spell *do*.

d o
d o

Circle each pair of flowers that has *do*.

119

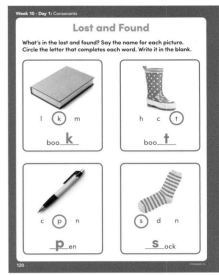

Lost and Found

What's in the lost and found? Say the name for each picture. Circle the letter that completes each word. Write it in the blank.

l (k) m
boo **k**

h c (t)
boo **t**

c (p) n
p en

(s) d n
s ock

120

Jars of Jam

Skip-count the jars. Write the missing numbers.

Count by 2s.

6 8 10 12 14 16 18

Count by 5s.

15 20 25 30 35 40 45

Count by 10s.

30 40 50 60 70 80 90

121

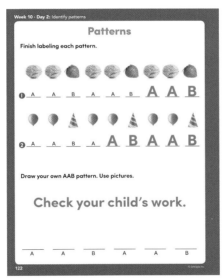

Patterns

Finish labeling each pattern.

❶ A A B A A B   **A A B**

❷ A A B A   **A B A A B**

Draw your own AAB pattern. Use pictures.

Check your child's work.

A   A   B   A   A   B

122

Missing Letters

Add a letter to complete the name of the object in each picture.

do **g**

c ube

b **i** ke

c **a** ke

p ig

ca **t**

b **e** d

r ose

123

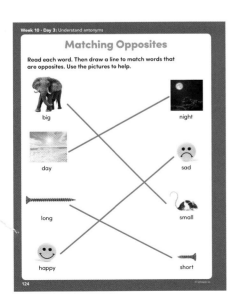

Matching Opposites

Read each word. Then draw a line to match words that are opposites. Use the pictures to help.

big

day

long

happy

night

sad

small

short

124

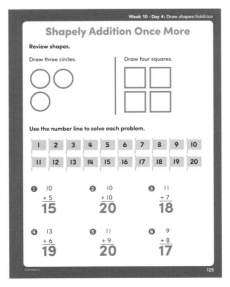

Shapely Addition Once More

Review shapes.

Draw three circles.

Draw four squares.

Use the number line to solve each problem.

| 1 | 2 | 3 | 4 | 5 | 6 | 7 | 8 | 9 | 10 |
| 11 | 12 | 13 | 14 | 15 | 16 | 17 | 18 | 19 | 20 |

❶ 10
+ 5
15

❷ 10
+10
20

❸ 11
+ 7
18

❹ 13
+ 6
19

❺ 11
+ 9
20

❻ 9
+ 8
17

125

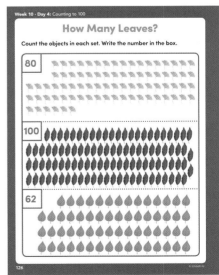

How Many Leaves?

Count the objects in each set. Write the number in the box.

80

100

62

126

Missing Vowels

Add a vowel to each puzzle to make two words.
Use the pictures as clues.

A Noise

Read the story. Then, answer the questions.

Li and Aya were walking home.
They passed a tall tree.

The girls heard a spooky noise.
Was it crying? They stopped walking.
They held hands.

Then Aya smiled and pointed up.
"Look!" she said.

Li saw the kitten. "Oh, kitty!"
said Li. "We will get help for you."

❶ Why did the girls hold hands?
○ to cross a street
○ Li was crying
● to feel safer

❷ What made the noise? _a kitten_

127

128

FOR OUTSTANDING ACHIEVEMENT

CONGRATULATIONS!

This certificate is awarded to

I'm proud of you!